Jayne Persico presents...

Innovative Adornments

An Introduction to Fused Glass & Wire Jewelry

Wardell

PUBLICATIONS INC

This is an example of a "bead" style watch band. These unique tropical fish beads were made for me by my friend and fellow glass artist Don McKinney.

Cataloging in Publication Data
  Persico, Jayne
Innovative Adornments - An introduction to Fused Glass & Wire Jewelry /
Author: Jayne Persico; jewelry design & fabrication, Jayne Persico;
Includes index.
ISBN 0-919985-35-1
    1. Glass jewelry. I. Title.
NK5440.J48P47 2002   748.8   C2002-902753-5

Printed in Thailand by Phongwarin Printing Ltd.

Published simultaneously in Canada and USA

E-mail: info@wardellpublications.com

Website: www.wardellpublications.com

Jayne Persico presents...

Innovative AdornmentS

Author
Jayne Persico

Text Editor
Stuart Goldman

Jewelry Design & Fabrication
Jayne Persico

Photography
Bill Reshetar Photography
and
Glenwood Jackson Photography

Book Layout & Typography
Randy Wardell

Publisher
Randy Wardell

Acknowledgements

A special thanks to Dody Ottaviani for being a great assistant but more importantly for being my best friend; Don McKinney for creating incredible fish beads for my wire designs, Eric Lovell for sharing his knowledge on compatibility; The Uroboros Glass Studios, Coatings by Sandberg, The Bullseye Glass Co. and Spectrum Glass Co. for their support and contributions to my classes; my son Tino for assisting me at the computer, Helen and Fran McGaugh, Monica Barrett, my students at the Hazleton Art League; Howard Deis for introducing me to glass; and last but not least my family for their love and support. A special thank you to my friend and Publisher Randy Wardell for making this book a wonderful experience!

Published by

Wardell
PUBLICATIONS INC

To receive our electronic newsletter or to send suggestions please contact us
by E-mail: info@wardellpublications.com or visit our Website: www.wardellpublications.com

A Message from the Author

I have been working with art glass for more than 35 years and during that time I've researched and experimented with a wide range of techniques and traditions. Eventually my experience in stained glass crossed paths with my long-lived love of jewelry design. It was then that I delightfully discovered the opportunity to create art glass jewelry. Blending my practical knowledge in both fields, I developed a process to combine glass-fusing components with semi-precious stones using wire-wrapping techniques. At the same time I perfected a unique process to create kiln formed bracelets. In addition to these new accomplishments I also developed a line of tools to make the forming tasks easier. As an artist and long time instructor it gives me great pleasure to share my jewelry making methods with you through this book, Innovative Adornments.

In fact, this book was written largely in response to the requests of my students. Despite the intensity of the many classes I conduct throughout the country, many students express a desire for more instruction time, additional guidance, motivational hints and refreshers that we just don't get to cover before class

time runs out. Innovative Adornments is my way of sharing these important themes with my new students and my familiar friends, one-on-one, at your pace, on your schedule and in the comfort of your own creative environment.

The techniques you will learn here have been tried, tested and enjoyed in my workshops both in the U.S. and Internationally over the past fifteen years. But beyond the 'how-to' approach of the book, I hope you will come away with new ideas that will lead to a personal exploration in glass. It is my wish for you to discover that special cycle of inspiration and accomplishment repeating itself in all you do. Thank you for allowing me to being a part of your creative journey.

Jayne Persico

This brooch was created using a triangle shaped piece of dichroic glass and pearl beads strung on fine gold wire. It is also accented with a pear shaped amethyst in lower center and a round citrine at top right.

Author Contact Information:

J. P. Glassworks Studio
50 North Vine Street
Hazleton, PA 18201 USA
E-Mail: jayne@jpglassworks.com
Website: www.jpglassworks.com

TABLE OF CONTENTS

A Message From the Author 4

Chapter 1   Introduction: Getting Started On The Glass Fusing Process 6
Chapter 2   Compatible Glass: What It Is And Why You Need It 7
Chapter 3   Glass Tools, Supplies & Techniques 8
             Glass Cutters 8
             Scoring and Breaking Glass 9
             Grinders and Bits 12
             Glass Saws 13
Chapter 4   Preparing Glass Cabochons 14
             Cutting, Shaping And Layering Components For Fusing 14
Chapter 5   Kiln Set Up and Firing 17
             Choosing Your Kiln 17
             Preparing the Kiln for Firing 18
             Safety Considerations for Kilns 21
             The Firing Process 22
Chapter 6   Wire Wrapping Tools and Supplies 23
             Pliers 23
             Drills, Wire, and Beads 24
             Adhesives for Cold Fusing 25

THE PROJECTS

Chapter 7   Pendants 26
  Project 1   Channel Mount Pendant 30
  Project 2   Notched Channel Mount Pendant 32
  Project 3   Simple Hanging Loop Pendant 34
  Project 4   Notched and Drilled Pendant 36

Chapter 8   Watchbands 38
  Project 1   Cabochon Watchband 40
  Project 2   Bead Watchband 44

Chapter 9   Bracelets 47
  Project 1   Cabochon Bangle Bracelet 50
  Project 2   Bead Bangle Bracelet 54

Chapter 10   Pins and Brooches 57
  Project 1   Angel Pin Brooch 60

Chapter 11   Rings 64
  Project 1   Wire Wrapped Cabochon Ring 66

Chapter 12   Earrings 72

Index   Find What You're Looking For 78

Chapter 1

Introduction
Getting Started On The Glass Fusing Process

Jewelry making is the perfect place to get started on learning the glass fusing process. Kiln working is very forgiving on the smaller scale and will allow you to gain experience and confidence while building a solid foundation for progressing to any other levels of endeavor. If you are already an experienced fuser, Innovative Adornments can only enhance your options by adding a new creative outlet for your craft.

Fusing is, at its most basic, stacking two or more layers of glass in a kiln and heating the glass until it is blended or joined into a single unit. Different effects or levels of fusing are achieved by adjusting the temperature and length of time the glass is in the kiln. However, in order to fuse successfully, the glass pieces

This photo shows examples of various colors of standard fusing glass with a COE of 90 (see sticker at center, back)

must be compatible with one another. Compatible means the glass will expand and contract at the same rate when it is heated and cooled. There are many types and formulations for glass and most are not fusing compatible with each other. Glass manufacturers recognized this was a problem for artists and devised a test for co-efficient of expansion (commonly referred to as COE) - which is the standard measurement of expansion of the heated glass - and now label the compatibility of the glass for your convenience (see photo of these labels on page 7). This tested compatible sticker insures perfect fusing every time. The availability of tested compatible glass makes today's fusing relatively simple.

The Uroboros Glass Studios and The Bullseye Glass Company both manufacture a line of 90 COE fusing glass that is compatible with each other. The Uroboros

Glass Studios also manufactures a separate line of 96 COE fusing glass that is compatible with a line of 96 COE glass from The Spectrum Glass Company. The latter is marketed under the name "System 96".

Fusing glass is available in standard thickness (approximately 1/8" - 3mm) and thin (approximately 1/16" - 1.5 mm), and can be purchased in small 12"square (30 cm) 'hobby sheets' that are perfect for jewelry making. Due to its increasing popularity, the fusible glass palette is quite extensive, giving you a vast variety of colors to choose from. These colors can be opalescent or transparent, smooth or textured, and are also available in many iridescent and dichroic finishes.

This photo shows examples of Dichroic coated fusing glass with a COE of 90 (notice stickers on several pieces)

Dichroic glass is the most popular and effective glass for jewelry designing. Dichroic is a special coating placed on glass by using a highly technical vacuum deposition process. Originally produced for the aerospace industry, dichroic glass is now available to the artistic community as well. The main characteristic of dichroic glass is that it has a transmitted color and a completely different reflective color. These two colors shift and blend depending on your angle of view. With the play of light, together with its vibrant hues, dichroic glass is a prime tool used to add interest to any piece of work. Artists have an unlimited freedom of expression when working with dichroic glass.

Whatever glass you choose, the ultimate success of any piece of jewelry is what you, the craftsperson, put into it; the design, the choice of materials and your own skill in coordinating the steps and processes. The end result will always be due to your efforts!

Chapter 2

Compatible Glass
What It Is And Why You Need It

By Eric Lovell,
President of Uroboros Glass Studios, Inc

If you are planning on fusing more than one color or type of glass together you naturally want the results to survive your process and endure for years of use or display without cracking. The only way to get those results is to use glasses that are "compatible", or "fit", with each other in terms of physics. Glasses that are compatible have only minor stresses at the adjoining edges, while those that are not compatible have significant stresses upon cooling, (pressure as high as 800 lbs per square inch - 58 kg per square cm) certainly enough to start a crack or possibly shatter completely.

Glasses that are colored differently all have unique compositions, sometimes "very unique", depending on the specific color. In order to achieve their colors they have different ingredient compositions, so it follows that their physical characteristics such as thermal expansion (the amount they expand when heated) and their viscosity (gumminess) vary. These characteristics must be matched in order for fused glasses to be compatible to one another.

Examples of "Tested Compatible" glass with a COE of 90 manufactured by Uroboros Glass Co. (note sticker at left center)

From the earliest Ptolemaic fused mosaics and Egyptian sand core vessels to the French Pate-de-verre in the early 1900's, the only ancient glass works that have survived until today are those that were made with compatible glass component colors. You can be sure that many, many times the numbers of those that survive today were not so fortunate. They were lost to immediate or delayed breakage caused by incompatible component colors. Those that we still possess today were the result of accidental or deliberate compensating adjustments in the glass formulae by their makers;

adjustments that attempted to zero out the effect of the formula variations necessary to achieve the desired colors and still be viable after firing.

Today we have multiple options when selecting glass for mixed color glass fusing projects. You can find existing glasses, test the expansion characteristics yourself, and use only those that work together. You could make your own glass from scratch, and learn to make the compensating formula adjustments yourself. Or you can choose the easiest method; you can specify specially manufactured "Tested Compatible" glasses, now available in a broad array of colors, and in forms ranging from full sheets to containers of like-sized fragments called frits.

Since the mid-1980's specialty glass manufactures have done the technical work for you, making and marketing clearly labeled Tested Compatible glasses. A label certifying a Tested Compatible product means the manufacturer has tested the color and found it to have only minor stresses in most anticipated uses and when fused against a known standard. Does that mean you shouldn't do any testing? No. If your work is very valuable, or if your technique is unusual, I recommend fuse testing all component colors first in a facsimile of your final work. It's always better to uncover a potential problem in a trial piece than on your masterpiece the day you are hanging the show!

So, unless you are especially technically oriented, specify Tested Compatible Glass products. You'll gain the freedom to concentrate on the fun part of glasswork: color selection and design.

Samples of "Tested Compatible" stickers from various glass manufacturers. Look for these stickers to ensure all the glass you're buying can be successfully fused in the same project.

Chapter 3

Glass Tools, Supplies & Techniques
An Introduction To Basic Glassworking

Glass Cutters:

Despite the fact that inexpensive steel-wheeled glass cutters exist, the only glass cutters I recommend are those with professional quality carbide cutting wheels. For your convenience, safety and expenditure in both money and time, work with the best tools available. There are several models of glass cutters available, from the traditional pencil or barrel handles to the pistol-grip styles and numerous new ergonomic designs. Many cutters, both old and new, have a built in reservoir to hold the cutter lubricant. If you choose one that doesn't have this feature you will need to keep a container of cutting oil handy on your workbench. Oil will do three things; 1- it lubricates the cutter wheel, helping it to move along the glass smoothly; 2- it helps in the removal of microscopic glass shards that get caught in the wheel housing; 3- it keeps the glass score from 'curing' and makes breaking along the score easier. I feel it is important to try a variety of cutter styles before you make your purchase. Fortunately most retail art glass supply stores have demonstrator cutters that you can take for a test drive, so take advantage of this opportunity. The cutter handle grip that is the most comfortable in your hand and allows you to follow your pattern line effectively is the right cutter for you, bar none!

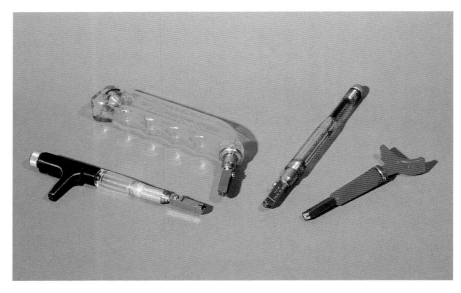

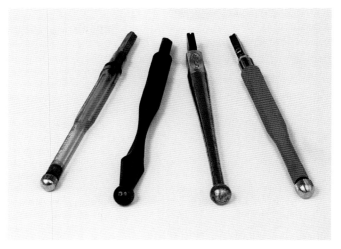

The 2 photos above show a selection of the professional quality glass cutters all with carbide cutting wheels

Gripping Styles and Methods:

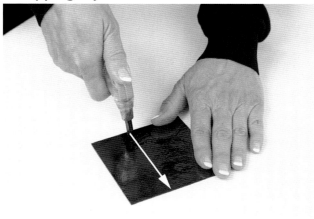

Pistol Grip Cutter (only one correct way to hold this model).

Holding the Glass Cutter:

Some types of glass cutters have only one correct way to grip them (for example, the pistol grip) while the traditional 'barrel' style cutter has a number of different ways to hold it. One grip is not necessarily better than the others, it really comes down to what feels right to your hand and most importantly which grip enables you to consistently make a steady and even score. Above all, the grip you use must stabilize the cutter to ensure the wheel is always perpendicular to the surface of the glass.

Hold the cutter like a pencil.

Hold the cutter in a clenched fist.

Scoring the glass:

The proper way to score glass is to apply a firm, even pressure straight down onto the cutter, while pushing it away from you across the surface of the glass. As with anything else it will take practice to get the sense for the correct pressure. While some people feel that pulling the cutter is the way to score, you will find this method could obscure the line you are tracing, which in turn causes problems with accuracy. Whatever method you settle on, you should feel the cutting wheel roll smoothly with a slight but even resistance as you slowly progress across the glass. If you hear a 'crackling' sound, you are pushing too hard. If the wheel is not turning, glass shards are clogging the cutting wheel, so soak it in oil and run it along a clean sheet of paper and you should see the glass fragments come out. This will be very important if your cutter has a 'wick' for depositing oil on the wheel. Always score the glass from one edge to another, allowing the wheel to roll gently off the far edge.

Safety Glasses:

As visual artists we must safeguard our eyes. So please, always wear safety glasses while cutting, grinding and drilling glass and when viewing hot glass in the kiln.

Keep them in your studio and use them!

You should have extra glasses on hand for your guests.

It is a good idea to practice your scoring and breaking on clear window glass (or any inexpensive colored glass scraps you have available) before attempting to cut your first project on good fusing glass. It's not that fusing glass is more difficult to cut, but why put yourself under that level of pressure when just starting out?

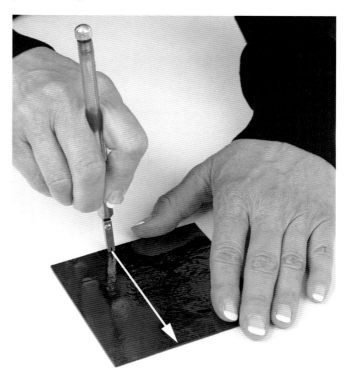

Hold the cutter between the index finger and middle finger.

Use a firm even pressure as you score across your glass piece from one edge to the other. You can score and break out gentle curves, but you cannot make an abrupt turn as you score.

Glassworking Pliers:

Glassworking pliers come in a variety of sizes and types. Each tool has its own specific function, although you can use some in a number of other capacities as well. Again, try out several and choose the types that work best for you. The following is a list of some of the most popular plier types.

1. Breaking Pliers - Metal pliers with a straight and wide jaw.

2. Narrow Jaw Grozing Pliers - Metal pliers with a narrow jaw and serrated teeth for smoothing away small bits of glass. Grozing pliers also come in wider widths, but for jewelry making purposes, this is the tool I recommend. (By the way, this was the 'grinder' before grinders were invented!)

3. Glass Snappers™ - Plastic pliers designed for straight cuts. Works especially well for breaking thin glass.

4. Ringstar™ **Runners** - Plastic pliers with a unique ring-jaw system to easily break out curved as well as straight line scores. This patented tool is the most versatile and easy to use of the all the running plier types.

5. Running Pliers - Plastic (shown) or metal (not shown) pliers designed for breaking out straight line cuts.

Breaking Out The Score:

Once you have scored the line with your glasscutter, select the pliers or breaker you find most comfortable and most appropriate for the job. Place your pliers on the far edge of the score, (where your score went off the glass) and with a firm but even pressure snap the glass apart. If done properly, the break will travel along the score exactly as planned.

Breaking with Hands Only - Place the glass between your thumb and curled index finger on both hands, making certain that the score line is centered equally between both thumbs on top of the glass, and that the second segment of your index fingers are aligned parallel to the score below. Now break the glass by first applying pressure by pulling outward (as if your trying to tear the sheet apart) and then snap downward (by rolling your knuckles) with an even pressure. This breaking method is recommended only for smaller pieces of glass (up to a of maximum 12" x 12" / 30 x 30 cm) until you have mastered this breaking technique.

Tip: It's easier to break the glass from the edge where you finished the score rather than from the edge where you started making the score.

4. Breaking With Hands Only

Using Breaking Pliers- place the jaws of the pliers perpendicular (at a 90° angle) to the score line. Hold the glass with one hand on the opposite side of the score line. Apply pressure by first pulling and then snap down with the pliers. Placing the pliers in the center of the component (as shown in the photograph) works fine for smaller pieces of glass, however when breaking longer scores place the pliers closer to the edge of the glass, at one the end of score.

Using Grozing Pliers - Small bumps or points left along the break can be nibbled away by 'pinching' them with the tip of the grozing pliers. You can also do some trimming by dragging the serrated edge downward over the points you want to remove. However this grozing technique should only be used for making small adjustments to reshape the edge of your glass piece. It is normally better to use your grinder to touch-up and smooth any rough edges.

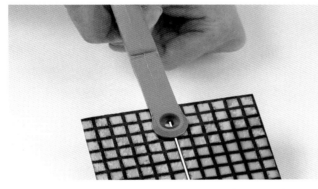 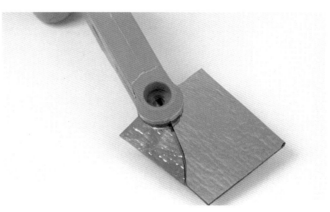

Using Ringstar™ Runners - Align the round opening in the top jaw of the pliers on the score line (no more than 3/4" - 2 cm, in from the edge of the glass) and gently squeeze the pliers. The glass will then break along the score line.

Ringstar™ runners work equally well when breaking out either straight or curved scores. The handle position in this case is not important, but aligning it with the score is a good habit to get into.

Using Running Pliers - Align the guide mark on the top of the running pliers with the score and gently squeeze the pliers. The handle should also line up as an 'extension' of the score to ensure proper alignment.

Using Glass Snappers™ - Align the guide mark on the top of the snappers with the score line. Gently squeeze the pliers and the glass will break along the score line. These pliers are ideal for breaking 1/16" (1.5-mm) extra thin glass.

Grinders and Bits:

One of the most indispensable power tools in today's glass shop is the grinder. Most of the glass grinding we need to do in jewelry making is to clean up rough edges and do some final shaping prior to kiln firing. Grinders come in a variety of types; most having a vertical shaft mounted grinder head, called a bit, and accessory attachments for straight edging and other needs. All grinders use a water based lubricant, usually applied through the sponge located behind the bit. It is important to keep the sponge clean and free of particles and to change the lubricant frequently.

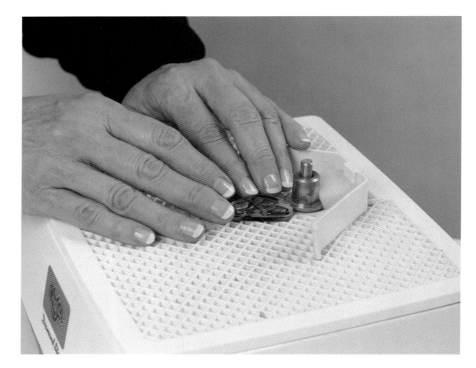

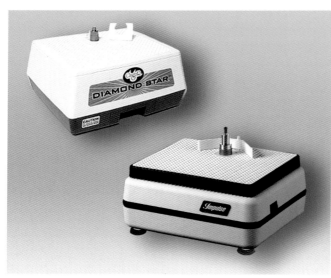

The above grinders are only two samples from the large assortment of hobby-duty grinder models that are available.

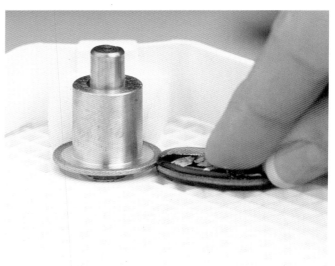

This close-up photo shows the Mika Jewelry Bit™ also called a channeling bit, being used on the perimeter of a cabochon.

The above grinders are fitted with the standard 3/4" medium grit diamond coated bit. This bit fulfills most needs for normal glass projects. Bits are also available in fine and coarse grits and in different sizes and profiles for specialized needs.

There are new innovations in grinder bits in the way they attach to the shaft, but be aware that not all bits fit all grinders, so make certain that any new bit or grinder accessory you purchase is compatible with your equipment.

Finally always wear eye protection when using a grinder; high speed glass particles can be hazardous.

A grinder is required to accomplish one very important wire-wrapped jewelry function called channel notching. In fact the wire-wrapped jewelry process would be impossible without this procedure.

The photo above shows a grinder fitted with the Mika Jewelry Bit™. This specialized bit is used to grind a shallow rounded channel (a slot) into the perimeter edge of a glass components. This channel will accommodate the wire 'frame' that is used to connect and hold the various components together in an assembled jewelry piece. This bit will fit the majority of grinders, but be sure to check with your grinder dealer before making your purchase.

Glass Saws:

Diamond glass saws can be described in 3 general categories. All of these saws work on standard household electricity, are portable, water-cooled and available from most glass retailers.

Wiresaws use a rigid wire-type blade with diamond particles embedded all around the blade, (not just on one edge).

There are 2 basic models in this category. One model, called a Ringsaw™ (photo upper right), has a cutting blade that is a rigid steel wire ring (think of a large "key-ring"). This is the saw that I used for the notching and scroll work in the projects for this book.

The other model, called a reciprocating saw (photo below right) uses a a straight wire blade that travels up and down very quickly.

Both models produce a similar result using the round (cylindrical) wire-type blade that has a diamond coating all the way around it. The advantage to this type of blade is the operator can actually move the glass in any direction they desire without having to turn it. For example, you could cut a slot straight into a piece of glass, then without stopping push the glass to the left, continuing to cut the slot 90° from the original line. In jewelry making this opens up a world of possibilities to create notches, scrolls, spirals and other shapes that would be extremely difficult, time consuming or even impossible with any other saw type.

Bandsaws photo right, use a steel ribbon blade with a diamond coated front edge to cut through the glass. There are several manufacturers of this type of glass saw and each model has its own distinctive features. Bandsaws are capable of cutting some fancy shapes and a practiced operator can achieve wonders with this type of saw.

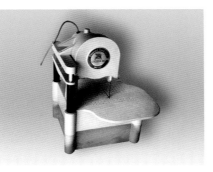

Tablesaws photo right, and **Cut-Off saws** (not shown) use a circular steel disk blade with a diamond coated edge to cut through the glass. This style of saw can only cut glass in a straight line. They are good saws that do come in handy in many glass shops but have limited capability for jewelry making.

Chapter 4

Preparing Glass Cabochons
Cutting, Shaping And Layering Components For Fusing

The cabochon is the basic fused element used in glass jewelry making. This photograph shows some of the variations of fused glass cabochons I create on a regular basis. I like to have an extensive selection available at all times. It's a good idea to create a minimum of 15 or 20 of these in various shapes, sizes and glass combinations to give yourself an exciting assortment to work with while doing the wire wrapping exercises in this book. Each project has a suggested size and shape of cabochon to work with (see the materials list in the front of each project,) so you may want to check those before making your samples. However, by creating a number of these without pre-planning your projects, the new cabochons themselves may inspire you by suggesting one thing or another.

1. Once you are comfortable cutting and breaking glass, you are ready to form and layer jewelry components. Determine the shape of the design and the glass color you want to use for the cabochon. Draw this shape onto the glass (or trace it from a paper pattern) with a waterproof marker.

2. The size and shape of the cabochon in this sample is approximately a 1-1/2"square. The base (bottom layer) will be cut from light pink. I've placed the shape on the corner of the glass so only two cuts will be needed to form it. The first cut will be a straight line from one side of the glass to the other (see arrow).

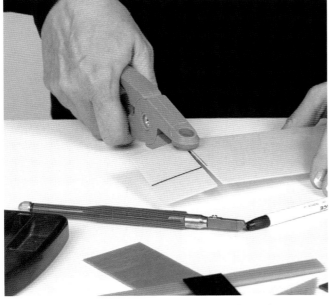

3. After you've made the first score, place the running pliers on the score line. Squeeze the pliers and the glass will break along the score line. We were all taught to break glass at the 'end' of a score, but when working with smaller pieces such as these, that is not always necessary, still, you should do what is comfortable for you.

4. The second cut is made by scoring along the remaining pattern line. If you are having problems scoring and breaking here's a little test you can try. Take a close look at your score. If there are small glass chips popping from the score line, or if the score appears very gritty, then you have exerted too much pressure on the cutter. The score should appear as a clean, even, faint white line. A note of caution; Never go over the same score twice as this will damage the cutter wheel and does not improve the score.

5. Use your breaking pliers (or Ringstar breakers as I am using in this photo). If there are any rough or uneven edges you could smooth them off using a glass grinder, but I think this is a good time to mention that it is not always necessary to have a perfect square shape or a precise size for this base piece. You will find that slight imperfections will smooth out during fusing. There is another reason as well; the truth is some badly cut and misshapen pieces become what we call "happy accidents" or "gifts of the glass gods"! So don't throw anything out, just think of inventive ways to use those accidental and bizarre shapes. When you are satisfied with the shape of the base piece, clean the glass by removing any marker lines, cutting oil residue and fingerprints.

6. After cutting the base piece of the design, cut smaller pieces for topical accents using contrasting colors and/or dichroic glass. Apply a small drop of white craft glue to secure these small design elements to the base. Be sure to use as little glue as possible, it is only used to prevent the glass from shifting while the piece is being placed on the kiln shelf. The glue will burn off in the kiln, but if you use too much glue it will leave a haze on the finished piece. Some people find that using glue diluted in water works very well and prevents 'build-up'.

7. You may find it is helpful to use tweezers to place the small design elements on the base piece. It is crucial that you keep fingerprints off the glass, as they will become permanently etched onto the glass during the fusing process.

Important note: When you have completed assembling this first set of cabochon blanks, set them aside until the glue is completely dry. Do not attempt to fuse these pieces while the glue is wet as the moisture could cause your pieces to crack while firing.

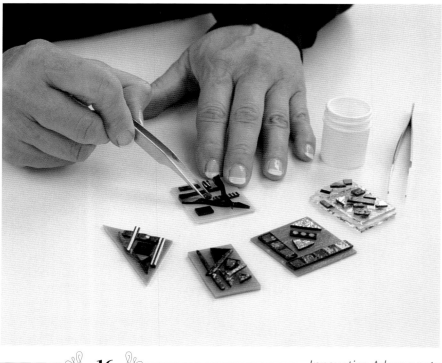

Chapter 5

Kiln Set Up and Firing
Choosing Your Kiln

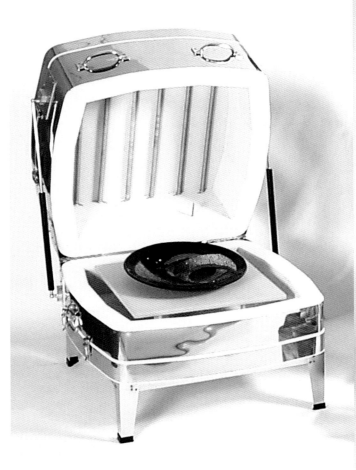

This kiln is a clam-shell type developed especially for glass fusing. It has a large capacity shelf that is 22" (56 cm) across.

This is a traditional style glass fusing kiln. It has elements both in the sides and the lid and holds a 16" (41 cm) kiln shelf.

There are several small portable kilns available that use ordinary 110 volt household electrical current. Only a few years ago this was not true, and when I was looking for my first portable kiln the choices were quite limited. Each of these new kilns have a different interior size, controls, features, and loading profiles, as well as price tag, so shop around for what you feel suits your overall needs. Aim Kilns manufactures the portable kiln that I have used for the projects in this book (see photo on page 18 at top left). It has an interior measurement of 8" x 8" x 4" deep. This kiln really cooks (pun intended) and heats up at a very fast rate. The relatively small pieces that we fire and use for jewelry can tolerate a fast "ramp-up" rate, however if you intend to fuse larger pieces you will need to increase the heat in a more controlled manner and quite frankly, it would also require a larger kiln. I

recommend that you get an introduction to fusing book for details on firing larger pieces.

I think it is important to note that the jewelry component pieces in this book can be fused in any size kiln. Larger kilns, such as the Skutt Clamshell (see photo above, left) will take longer to reach the fusing temperature and will cool at a slower rate but you can do many more pieces in one firing. Ramp times and temperature readings vary to some degree with every individual kiln so I strongly recommend that you test fire any kiln you intend to use and keep accurate records of all your fusing projects and firing profiles. This will be most helpful when you are trying to repeat a successful fusing project or possibly trying to avoid another 'disaster'.

Preparing the Kiln for Firing

Once you have selected your kiln, whatever size or model it may be, you must now prepare it for firing. You never place your glass for firing directly in a kiln. You must place it on a surface that can be inserted into and removed from the kiln itself; normally this will be a treated kiln 'shelf'. The shelf must be treated to resist (or release) the glass from adhering to it while molten. You can use materials such as fiberboard and kiln paper to act as the release, but the industry standard is the rigid clay shelf with kiln wash and we need to prepare it properly before placing our glass on it for fusing.

1. Kiln wash is an important 'tool' in the fusing process. It is a powdered resist material that is mixed with water and applied to a kiln shelf to keep the glass from sticking during firing. The kiln shelf shown in the photo has been fired several times. To maintain a smooth surface the old kiln wash has to be cleaned off the shelf and replaced periodically. The best way to do

This small portable kiln uses ordinary 110 volt household electrical current and heats up at a very fast rate. It has an interior measurement of 8″ x 8″ x 4″ deep. This is the kiln model that was used for most of the projects in this book.

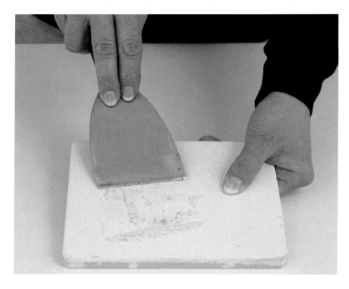

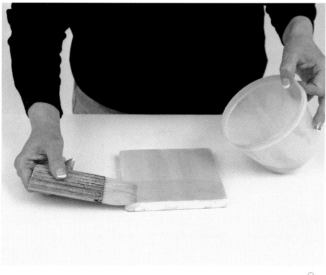

this is to scrape most of it off with a wide putty knife and then remove the remaining residue with a dry plastic-scouring pad. Wear a dust mask to protect yourself from any dust primer particles that become airborne.

2. Next we will apply a new layer of kiln wash. I use one part "Hi-Temp" kiln wash (a commercial product) to four parts cold water. Blend well (but do not allow bubbles to form, - if they do, let them subside before using the wash, otherwise they will leave tiny 'craters' when they dissipate) and apply the wash with a "hake" brush. The hake is an extremely soft and absorbent bristled brush used in Chinese ink painting, available at any good art supply store. Please note that there are a couple of types of hake brush; multiple headed like the one I use and a wide flat head as well. Either one will do the job. Load the brush with kiln wash and apply an even coat, "painting" it on in one direction only. When this first coat is dry (you can tell it's dry when the color has become pale) turn the shelf 90° and apply another coat of kiln wash in a cross direction. Apply at least 7 or 8 cross-alternating coats, always allowing sufficient time to dry between coats.

3. Some crafters dry the shelf between coats in a kiln set at a low temperature, but personally I find that if the shelf is left to air-dry between coats it will withstand many more firings before it needs to be scraped and prepped again.

4. When you have applied enough coats and the shelf is completely dry, smooth out any brush stroke texture by rubbing the surface lightly with the dry tip of your finger. If you do not smooth these tiny 'grooves' from the surface the remaining texture will be transferred to the backside of your fused cabochon.

5. I like to use 3 very different types (or levels) of kiln-firings in my jewelry pieces: They are tack fusing, full fusing, and fire polishing. This photograph shows examples of a tack fuse. Notice that the top design components remain slightly raised while it is melted just enough for the glasses to bond securely to each other. The edges are rounded and the surface has a gloss finish.

The temperature for a tack fuse ranges from 1400°F to 1500°F (760°C - 815°C). In a small kiln the temperature will be approximately 1450°F - 1500°F (790°C - 815°C). In a large kiln the temperature will be approximately 1400°F - 1450°F (760°C - 790°C).

6. This photograph shows examples of full fused cabochons. All layers of the glass have fully melted together resulting in a very smooth, glossy surface with a slightly convex shape. These cabochons are now ready to be incorporated into a finished jewelry piece.

The temperature for a full fuse ranges from 1450°F to 1600°F (760°C - 870°C). In a small kiln the temperature will be approximately 1500°F to 1600°F (815°C - 870°C) and in a large kiln the temperature will be approximately 1450°F to 1500°F (760°C - 815°C). These temperatures are averages only, you must test your kiln to determine the exact temperatures needed.

7. The last level is called fire polishing. This is done after an already fused glass piece has been 'cold worked' by cutting, grinding or shaping. The 4 ovals in the photo were created by cutting a full fused bar into 4 equal pieces. The pieces were shaped into ovals (on the grinder) and then fire polished to give them perfect gloss finish. Fire polishing is achieved at a temperature between 1325°F to 1500°F (720°C to 815°C).

Of course, all these temperatures are only a guide. You must test and log the results of your own kiln so that you know the exact temperature that is right for each of these three levels in the fusing process.

8. It is important to load a kiln with items that you intend to take to the same fuse level – either all tack fused or all full fused, etc. Also, each piece in the firing should have a similar number of layers; for example, it's fine to fire pieces together with one base layer and one or two element layers. However if you have pieces with one base layer, two element layers and a clear top layer, these would need to be fired in their own cycle. The key is to group items with a similar mass or volume together in a single firing or else some pieces will be over-fired while others could be under-fired all in the same load.

Note: The portable kiln shown in the photos on these pages is model 84J - Quick-Fire kiln manufactured by AIM Kilns. Size is 8"x8" x 4.5"(20 x 20 x 11.5cm) 120 volt/14 amp, w/infinite switch.

9. Sort your pieces according to layer/volume and arrange them on the kiln shelf. Make sure the pieces have sufficient room between them or they could 'spread out' at the highest temperature point during the firing and possibly stick to an adjoining piece expanding in its direction.

10. Place the kiln shelf and the pieces onto the base of the kiln. If you are using a larger style kiln, place the shelf into the kiln using 1"-high shelf posts. This will create a space between the kiln floor and the shelf to allow airflow under the shelf and help maintain a uniform temperature for your components. (If you are using an extremely large kiln like a bed kiln, be aware that there could be a temperature variance at different locations throughout the kiln. You must do test firings to find out what should be placed where.)

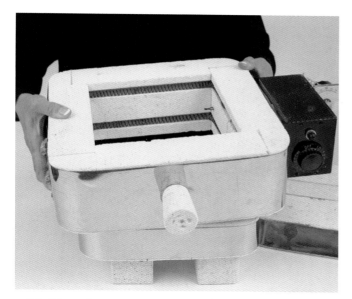

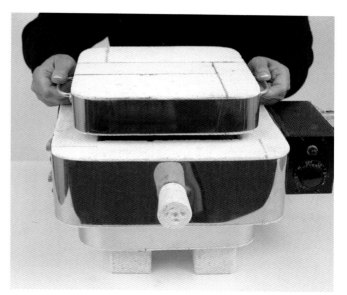

11. Place the center ring onto the base of the kiln (obviously you will skip this step if your kiln is permanently assembled).

12. Place the lid (top) on the kiln (or close the door) and plug the peep hold with the stopper.

13. Program your controller (if you have one) and/or start the fusing cycle (see schedule next page).

Safety Considerations For Kilns:

Although this may seem painfully obvious, allow me to be redundant in your own best interest - a kiln must be placed (secured and leveled) on a non-flammable surface and should be at least 18" away from any flammable walls or other items.

It is very important that you NEVER LEAVE A KILN UNATTENDED DURING THE FIRING PROCESS. You must be close by in the event of a serious occurrence, please don't take this risk – it's simply not worth it! Never use an extension cord to plug in your kiln. Kilns draw a large amount of electrical current and an extension cord that is not rated for the high current could overheat and cause a fire. If you have moved your kiln, make certain that your plug is firmly in the wall jack and that all the connections are secured and not frayed. If you have a new kiln, follow the instructions for more complete safety information. If you have a used kiln that came without an instruction booklet, contact the company that manufactured the kiln, they are normally happy to cooperate by supplying you with any necessary documentation to ensure that you safely enjoy using their equipment.

Power Light

Pyrometer

Infinite Switch

The Firing Process

The pieces we are firing for our purposes are small (approximately 2" x 2" - 5 x 5 cm or smaller) and that means you can turn the infinite switch to the high setting and leave it there until the desired temperature has been reached. Do not open the kiln before it has reached at least 1000 °F (540°C). Opening the kiln below this temperature usually triggers a thermal-shock that will shatter your pieces. Once the kiln is above 1000 °F (540°C) you can safely check the progress of the firing by lifting the lid (or opening the door) slightly to view the glass. Be sure to wear hi-temp kiln gloves and safety glasses to protect your hands and eyes from the heat and radiant glare. When the kiln has reached fusing temperature and the pieces have fused to the desired level, close (or replace) the lid securely, then turn the kiln off and allow it to cool to room temperature before removing your pieces. If you remove them too soon, this could also cause the pieces to crack or shatter. It is always better to allow too much time than too little.

If you are fusing pieces larger that 2" x 2" (5 x 5 cm) you must start the firing with the switch at the medium setting, allowing the kiln to heat slowly until it reaches between 800-900°F (425-485°C). This should take about 45-60 minutes. The slow heating permits the glass to heat evenly and prevent thermal shock. Once the kiln is above 900°F (485°C) you can safely turn the switch to the maximum setting until the fusing temperature has been reached.

Fusing glass pieces larger that the items we are using for jewelry requires a specific firing schedule based on the size, volume and thickness of glass. These pieces will need a longer firing time and will also require annealing and a slower cool-down schedule. There are some excellent books on glass fusing that you should reference for more information on other aspects of this exciting art form.

Chapter 6

Wire Wrapping Tools and Supplies
Items You Will Need For Wire Wrapping And Glass Shaping

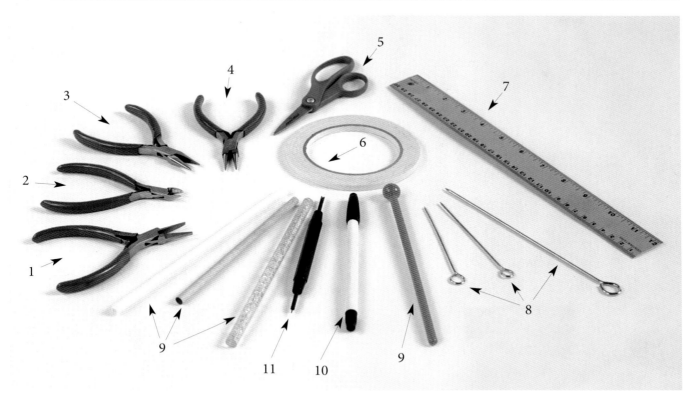

Essential tools used in wire wrapping:

Every aspect of glassworking and jewelry making calls for specialty tools to get the job done efficiently and correctly. Many of these tools have more than one use, while others are more specialized and their purpose is not 'transferable'.

You may already have some of the tools listed in this chapter on hand in your toolbox, or you may find them elsewhere around your home or in your studio. Some of the listed items are redundant (for instance you will find several dowels listed made from various materials). Please take the time to ensure you have all the proper implements on hand when you begin a project so that you will not have to stop in the middle and go shopping. To assist you with this, every project begins with a list of tools and materials that will be required.

1. Flat Nose Pliers - these pliers have 'wider' flat tines used to form sharp angles, hold multiple wires and straighten kinks that might develop when wire wrapping.

2. Flush Cutters – also referred to as wire cutters, are used to cut all jewelry wire.

3. Needle Nose Pliers – are pliers with 'narrower' flat-bottomed jaw pliers used to hold wire, to grip ends of wire and bend wire.

4. Round Nose Pliers - used to create loops in jewelry wire.

5. Short nosed scissors - standard scissors will work just as well, but either one should be kept available at all times with your other supplies.

6. Quilter's tape or narrow masking tape.

7. Metal Ruler - 12 inch (30 cm)

8. Metal Skewers - 3/64", 1/6", & 1/8" (1.2, 1.6, & 3.2 mm) used to form small loops & coils (used when a dowel is too big for the task).

9. Dowels - plastic and wood in various sizes, used to form loops and/or coils. You will want to collect sizes beginning with at least 1/8" to 1/2" (3.2mm to 1.3cm) diameter and possibly bigger.

10. Marking Pen (fine point)

11. Watch Tool - used to remove/install watch band pins, available through from craft or jewelry suppliers.

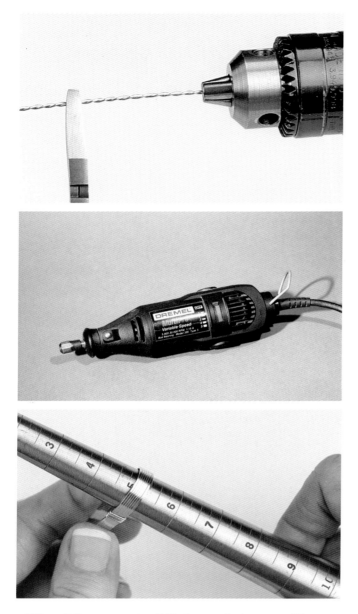

Additional Tools And Supplies

Drill, Standard (variable speed electric or cordless): This photo shows how the drill is used to twist 2 lengths of gold wire into one decorative strand. Notice how the flat nose pliers are used to hold the wire while twisting with the drill at low speed. You could also hold the end of the wires in a vise or wrap them around a nail driven into your workbench, however the latter will waste a couple inches of wire every time you use that method.

Dremel™ Drill Tool (high-speed – 20,000 rpm model, electric): with 5/64" (2mm) hollow core diamond drill bit. This photograph shows the hand held the Dremel tool. Use it with the diamond coated bit to drill holes in the glass components. Special note: The hollow core diamond drill bit is a specialty item that must be purchased from a glass supplier (it is not a standard Dremel bit), be sure to ask specifically for a "hollow core diamond drill bit" for glass.

A Ring Mandrel: This is a tapered rod (some have a built-in stand) with standard ring sizes clearly marked along its length. All custom jewelers use the mandrel to accurately form a ring at a predetermined size.

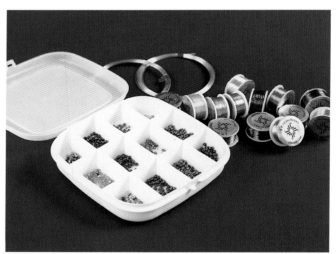

Wire: Wire comes in differing variations, profiles and workability (hardness). The larger coils at the top of this photograph are Solid Gold but similar profiles are available in Gold filled, Sterling Silver, Pure Silver, and other precious metal varieties. The bobbin coiled wire is copper wire that is available with an extensive variety of color coatings. When purchasing wire, be aware that it is sold in widths called 'gauges'. Also know that the greater the gauge number the narrower the width, and conversely the smaller the number the thicker the width. This is the opposite of what we are used to dealing with! For our purposes, we will be working with gauges 21 through 28 in most of our jewelry designs. Wire-wrapping wire also comes in many hardnesses- soft, quarter-hard, half-hard, three-quarter-hard, and full-hard. For projects in this book, we will be using half-hard gold and silver wires and colored copper wires that come in only one hardness.

Beads. The white sectioned box contains a collection of small-sized glass beads. Beads are available in many shapes, sizes, colors and materials and can be used in numerous ways to enhance our jewelry creations. You can make your own glass beads by a variety of methods, including fusing and by learning torchworking. They are also available in art glass stores, specialty bead stores, and arts & crafts retail stores. Beads are sold by type of material and the sizes are normally specified in millimeters.

Fused Glass Cabochons and Nuggets: This photograph shows an assortment of glass cabochons and nuggets that I created in my kiln using the technique described in Chapter 4 on page 14-16. These components are also available pre-made from a variety of sources, but it is much more fun to create your own unique shapes and designs. Remember, even your worst 'mistakes' can be re-shaped with saws and grinders and possibly re-fired with other components to become something useful and beautiful!

Adhesives For Cold Fusing

I like to call this process "cold-fusing", which is nothing more than applying a variety of design elements using adhesives. I use a variety of adhesives to attach items such as brooch pin-backs, earring studs, and other findings. It's also used to fasten supplementary decorative touches like faceted jewels, wire ribbons, pearls, as well as other glass component pieces. We are fortunate to have some rather miraculous bonding compounds available to us today; we're no longer 'gluing' now we're 'cold-fusing'!

The 2 basic categories of adhesives that I use in jewelry making are air-dry and ultra-violet light cured. My favorite air-dry adhesives are Bond 527 and E6000. Both of these cements will bond metal and other rigid items to glass and they also dry clear. There are, of course, many other effective adhesives that would work just as well but I have found these tow take care of most bonding needs. The same basic rules apply for both compounds. The area to be attached must be clean and dry and after they have been attached they must be left undisturbed for the proper curing time.

The other category of adhesive that I use is call UV or UltraViolet cement. This material will also bond most rigid items to one another but has the advantage of curing almost instantly when it is exposed to an ultraviolet light source. Natural sunlight does have a UV component but rarely accomplishes more than a 10% 'cure' rate. For 100% adherence, UV adhesives must be set or cured with an ultraviolet lamp made just for this purpose. It is also important that any surfaces to be joined with UV glues be absolutely and perfectly clean of any contaminant's such as, dust, marker inks, skin oils, or fine particles of any kind.

Air-dry adhesives will bond metal and other rigid items to glass

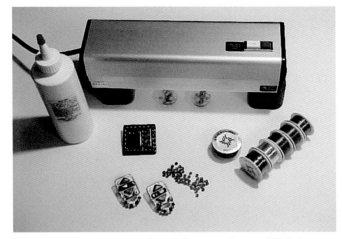

UltraViolet cement cures when it is exposed to an UV light

Scrub your glass and any components that are to be joined together with a cleaner containing rubbing alcohol or use the special cleaner available from the UV cement manufacturer.

Chapter 7
Pendants

It is curious how the components of glass and wire, as individual raw materials, can seem so mundane and yet when combined as wire wrapped glass jewelry are so strikingly attractive. This is one of those instances when the old adage; "It's not what you have, but how you use it" is really true. The pendants illustrated in these photographs were fabricated using the most basic of all wire wrapping techniques.

Chapter 7
Pendants

Chapter 7
Pendants

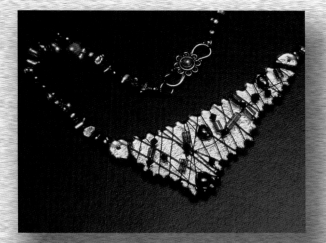

Chapter 7
Pendants

Channel Mount Pendant

TOOLS:

- Grinder with channeling bit
- Quilter's tape or narrow masking tape
- Drill for wire twisting
- Steel ruler
- Flush Cutters (Wire cutters)
- 1/8" Dowel (wood or plastic)
- Needle Nose pliers

MATERIALS:

- Cabochon- two layers, full fused glass, about 3/16" (5mm) thick and 1 1/2"- long by 1"-wide (3.8 x 2.5cm) see example of the one I used in photo at right
- 24 gauge, half hard, gold-filled round wire
- Gold mesh chain necklace with hook-eye clasp or any necklace cord or chain that can support the weight of this pendant

Channel mounting is a simple and elegant way to set glass jewelry to embrace and enhance its beauty. Yet, despite its sophisticated looks, the techniques required are uncomplicated and so it is a good place for us to begin. Each project chapter will begin with a listing of tools and materials, please make sure that you have everything on hand before you begin to avoid needless delays, as with all endeavors that involve learning new hands-on skills, there is a rhythm that we will try to achieve.

This elegant pendant is a great place to start our adventure in wire wrapped jewelry.

1. Use your grinder fitted with the Mika jewelry 'channeling' bit (see page 12 for more details on this process) to grind a channel around the entire perimeter edge of the glass cabochon. The channel should be just deep enough for the wire to hold the glass securely but not so deep that the wire can't be seen from the front view of the pendant.

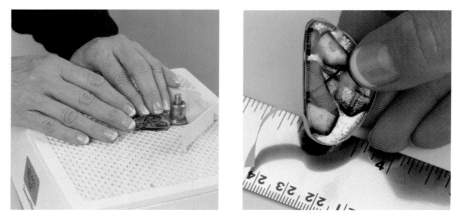

2. Measure the outside perimeter of the glass by wrapping Quilter's tape (or narrow masking tape) around the outside edge of the glass. Mark the tape with a felt pen where it meets itself. Remove and lay the tape flat on your work surface and measure the distance to get the circumference of your glass piece.

3. Add 6" (15 cm) to the circumference measurement (to allow for the hanging loop) and cut two pieces of wire to this length. Put the wires together and insert one end into the drill chuck and tighten to hold the wire firmly. Now hold the drill in one hand and use the flat nose (or needle nose) pliers in the other hand to hold the opposite end of the wires. Finally slowly pull on the drill's trigger and keep it at a very low speed to maintain control and achieve a perfect twist. Twisted wire is available commercially from jewelry suppliers but I like to create exactly what I need from my own stock of wire gauges & sizes.

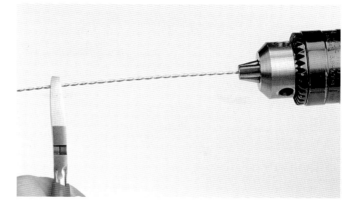

Note: When twisting two wires use 24-gauge wire, for three wires use 26-gauge wire and for four wires use 28-gauge wire.

4. Place the bottom center point of the cabochon over the center point of the twisted wire, checking to make certain that the twisted wire is securely seated in the channel. Work the wire into the channel around both sides of the pendant. now use the needle nose pliers to pinch and hold the two wires together at the top.

5. Continue to hold the wires with the pliers and slowly rotate the glass creating a twist in the wire at the top of the pendant. Make 1 1/2 to 2 revolutions only. If you over-rotate the glass you run the risk of snapping the wire or damaging the glass. As you twist you can feel the wire firm up, this is your signal to stop.

6. Place a dowel behind the wires at approximately 1/4" (6 mm) from the top of the pendant. Now wrap each wire around the dowel twice. The wires should be behind the dowel and pointing down. Bring these two wires around to the front, cross them over one another and wrap them around to the back of the pendant.

7. Remove the dowel and use your flush cutters to close clip the excess wire. Firmly crimp the ends 'into' the twist with your needle nosed pliers. To do this properly the wire ends need to be buried in twisted wire shank to ensure they won't scratch or snag clothing.

8. Here we see the finished pendant. Clean it using a mild soap and water mixture then thread it onto an appropriate neck chain to complete the project.

Notched Channel Mount Pendant

TOOLS:

- Grinder with channeling bit
- Ring saw or grinder with 1/8" (3.2mm) pin-type bit
- Quilter's tape
- Masking tape
- Metal ruler
- Flush Cutters (Wire cutters)
- Needle nose pliers
- 1/4" (6mm) dowel

MATERIALS:

- Glass component - choose a cabochon that is two layers, full-fused 3/16" (5 mm) thick, and about 3/4" x 2" (2 x 5 cm) see photo
- 22 gauge round black wire
- Beads – 3/16" (5 mm) clear glass (or a bead type and color to match the cabochon)
- Beaded necklace (or any necklace type that you prefer)

By doing an easy alteration on the basic cabochon and adding some beads, you will have created a much more complicated looking piece of jewelry with very little additional effort. The beads will be added to the perimeter wire as a decorative element and will appear to 'float' in the notched spaces.

It's easy to add a few notches and fill them with small beads during wire wrapping.

1. Notch the left side of the cabochon six times. I prefer to use the Taurus II Ringsaw™ for notching and cutting cabochons. As an alternative you could use your grinder fitted with a small (1/8") "pin type" bit or use a bandsaw or wiresaw (see page 13 for details). Create the first notch and check the size of the notch to make sure it will easily accommodate the beads you have selected. Once you have established the correct notch size finish the other five notches by spacing them evenly along the edge. Depending on the size of the cabochon it may only need 5 notches or perhaps 7 or 8 notches would be better – you be the judge.

Professional Tip:

Fire polish your cabochon to remove the saw blade marks and put a high polish on all edges. Simply place the cabochon back in the kiln and fire it to 1400°F (750°C). See page 19 - item 7, for more details.

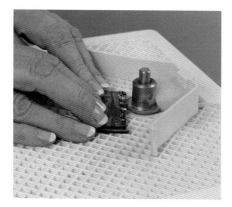

2. Next we need to grind a channel into the perimeter edge of the glass cabochon using the Mika jewelry bit as we did in the previous project. You must use extra care as you grind the channel into the delicate "peak" areas between the notch spaces. These points are fragile and can easily chip or break if too much pressure is applied.

3. Measure the cabochon's circumference using quilter's tape (as we did in project 1, step 2). Cut a length of 22 gauge wire about 6" (15 cm) longer than the circumference. Then locate and mark the center point of the wire.

4. Place the center point of the wire in the channel at the center bottom of the cabochon. Wrap the wire around the pendant's perimeter making sure the wire is fully seated in the channel. Secure the wire on the right side and bottom with masking tape to hold it in place. Finally thread the beads onto the wire and fit each one into a notch point on the side of the pendant.

5. Wrap the wire around the top corners of the cabochon, check that it is fully seated in the perimeter channel then pinch the two wires together at the top of the pendant with needle nosed pliers.

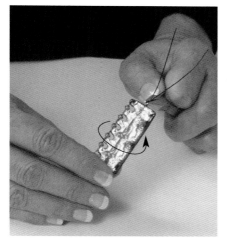

6. Continue to hold the wires with the pliers and rotate the glass 1 1/2 to 2 revolutions to secure the wire at the top of the pendant. Be careful that you don't over tighten the wire. Too much twist pressure could break the wire or worse damage the glass cabochon. As you twist you can feel the wire firm up, this is your signal to stop.

7. Place the 1/4" (6 mm) dowel behind the wires, about 3/16" (5 mm) up from the top of the cabochon. Wrap them once over the dowel from front to back.

8. Continue to wrap the wires around the dowel and bring them to the front. Cross them over the front and bend them around to the back of the pendant.

9. Close clip the excess wire with your wire cutters, then use the needle nose pliers to firmly crimp the ends flush to the backside of the pendant.

10. This photo shows the finished pendant. Use mild soap and water to clean it then string it onto a necklace chain for final presentation.

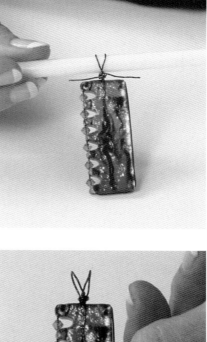

Innovative Adornments

Simple Hanging Loop Pendant

TOOLS:

- Shallow plastic container
- Micro foam (used for packing glass for shipping and should be available at your glass retailer or any packaging/mailing center)
- Dremel™ Flex-shaft with 5/64" (2 mm) hollow core diamond drill bit
- Metal ruler
- Flush cutter (Wire cutter)
- Metal cooking skewer - 5/32" (4 mm) dia.
- Needle nose pliers

MATERIALS:

- Glass component -choose an oval or triangle shaped cabochon that is two layers, full-fused 3/16" (5 mm) thick, and about 1" x 1-3/4" (2.5 x 4.5 cm). Or choose any shape or size cabochon that you prefer.
- 21-gauge sterling silver or gold-filled round wire, half-hard
- Water -(for cooling the glass and drill bit)
- Leather cord necklace with hook-eye clasp or any complimentary necklace

1. Pre-drilling set-up: Line a shallow plastic container with a piece microfoam sheet and enough cold water to cover the foam to a depth of about 3/8" (1 cm). Lay the glass cabochon on top of the foam, front side up. Make sure the glass is completely underwater so both it and the diamond bit will maintain a cool temperature during the drilling. Push down on the glass firmly with your fingers the foam will help you to hold the glass securely while drilling.

2. Drill the hole with the Dremel using a 5/64" (2 mm) hollow core diamond drill bit. Always drill using the highest speed (yes, I said "high!") on a setting of at least 20,000 revolutions per minute!

Special Note: A standard drill (like the one we use for twisting wire) has speeds much slower than a Dremel drill and will not work satisfactorily to drill holes. Due to the slower speed, if you try to use a hollow core diamond bit in a standard drill the diamond coating will fatigue quickly and ruin the bit.

Don't let the word 'simple' fool you. Although this process has fewer steps than other projects this project requires drilling a hole through the glass. It's not a difficult skill to learn but does require some practice. Try it a couple of times on some scrap glass before committing to the cabochon you want to use.

Do not try to hurry the drilling process by pressing down. The weight of the drill machine will be sufficient to enable the hollow core diamond bit to bore through the glass.

Tip: When drilling with a Dremel tool do not apply downward pressure on the glass, as the weight of the drill will be sufficient to cut through the glass. Patience will be your greatest helper while drilling. Just hold the drill bit in that same spot without pressing down and let the Dremel drill do the work.

3. Cut approximately 4" (10 cm) of the round wire you've selected for this projects. Use needle nose pliers to bend the wire at the center to form a U shape as shown in the photo at right.

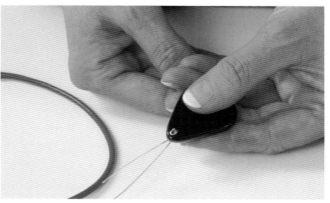

4. Again use the needle nose pliers to form a hook at the central bend point.

5. Insert the loose ends of the wire through the hole from the back to the front, leaving the hook on the backside of the pendant.

6. Place the 5/32" (4 mm) skewer against the wire from the back and wind both wires around it to shape the hanging loop.

7. Remove the dowel and cut the wires a little longer than the loop.

8. The leather cord necklace I am using for this project has a large clasp on both ends. This means I will need to insert the necklace cord before I tighten and crimp the wire loop (see note at the end of instructions). Once the cord is in place, thread both wire ends into the first loop on the back of the pendant. Crimp and secure it flush to the loop with the needle nose pliers.

9. The last photo shows the back of the finished pendant. Notice how the wire ends are crimped and flattened neatly. If necessary clean the pendant with a mixture of mild soap and water.

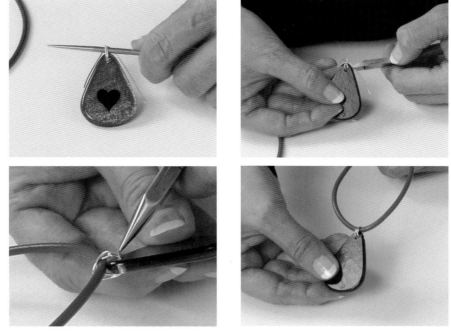

Note: The last two steps were completed while the pendant was on the leather necklace because the large clasp would not fit through the hanging loop, which was sized for the leather cord. If you have selected an alternative necklace with a small clasp, then these two steps will not have to be completed with the necklace in place.

Notched and Drilled Pendant

TOOLS:

- Ring saw, band saw or grinder with 1/8" (3.2mm) pin-type bit
- Dremel™ Flex-shaft with 5/64" (2 mm) hollow core diamond drill bit
- Metal ruler
- Flush cutter (Wire cutter)
- Needle nose pliers
- Metal skewer, 5/32" (4 mm)

MATERIALS:

- Cabochon, rectangle, two layers full fused glass, approximately 3/4" x 2" (2 x 5 cm)
- 21 gauge round Sterling silver or gold wire, half-hard
- 30 glass beads in assorted colors, 1/16" (2 mm) dia.
- Leather necklace with hook-eye clasp or any

With this pendant we get an opportunity to combine the techniques we learned in projects 2 & 3, plus we'll add a new flourish for visual interest. The results are quite sophisticated as you can see.

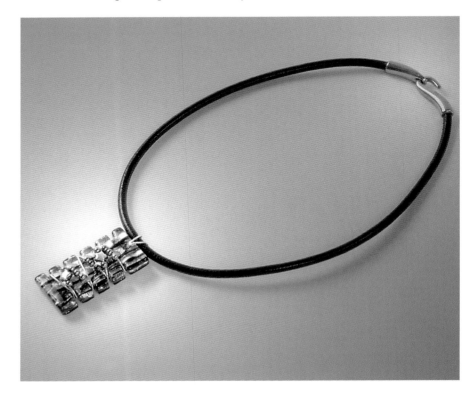

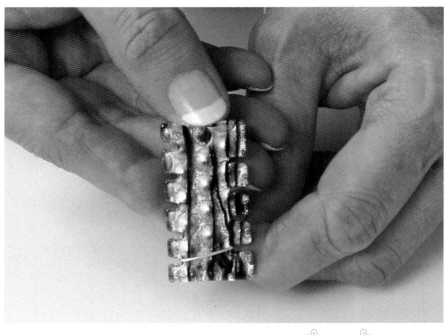

1. Drill a hole at the top center of the cabochon (follow the procedure in project 3 page 34)

2. Create five notches on the left side of the cabochon and four notches on the right side. Be sure to stager the notches from one side to the other. These notches do not have to accommodate beads (as they did in project 2) so they can just be the width of the ring saw or band saw blade or the pin-type grinder bit. Fire polish the cabochon, see tip on page 37.

3. Cut a 14" (35 cm) length of 21 gauge wire. Center the wire across the front and near the bottom portion of the pendant.

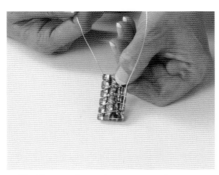

4. Wrap the wire around the pendant by looping it back through the two lowest notches on both sides and bend it around to the back.

5. Cross the wires securely across the back and bring the wires around to the front through the next two higher notches.

6. Thread 3 or 4 the beads onto one of the wires and position them across the front of the pendant. Wrap the wire around the pendant through the next two higher notches, cross them on the back and repeat the beading/bending process until you have reached the upper-most notch set.

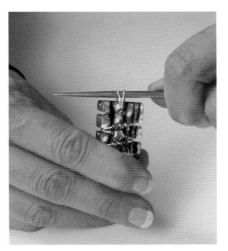

7. Make sure the final wrap leaves the wires at the back of the pendant.

8. Insert both wires through the drilled hole from the back to the front of the pendant.

9. Place the skewer (or dowel) behind the wires and wrap them around the dowel from the front to the back.

10. Remove the skewer and insert the necklace into the loops before closing them off (same as we did in the last project). Clip the wires leaving them a little past the top wire that crosses the back. Use needle nose pliers to form a hook on the ends both wires.

11. Thread these hooks under the top cross wire and crimp them securely. Clean with a mixture of mild soap and water.

PROFESSIONAL TIP - FIRE POLISHING

If you really want to put some professional polish to your pendants you will need to add an extra step after you have notched and drilled the cabochon.

Fire polishing will smooth the saw blade, grinder and diamond drill marks and put a high polish on all these edges.

After you have drill the hole, created the notches or modified the shape in any way simply place the cabochon back in the kiln and fire it to 1400°F (750°C). See page 19 - item 7, for more details.

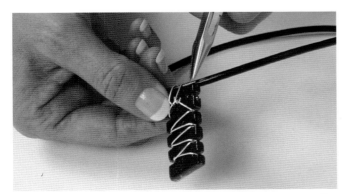

Chapter 8
Watches

A watch has the distinction of being the personal adornment that is most often 'looked at' by the wearer. A watch is a necessary accessory for many people and is often the only jewelry some people wear. Still, it doesn't have to be 'plain', does it? In creating the glass watchbands, it is my wish that the beauty of the piece serve to remind the wearer to stop and see the beauty of the world around them; to notice that common and ordinary things can be wonderful. To put it another way, the form can succeed beyond the function!

Chapter 8
Watches

Cabochon Watchband

This watchband project takes advantage of many of the procedures you acquired in the prior chapter and will also introduce some new techniques for wire wrapping, so let's begin!

TOOLS:

- Glass cutter (or Glass saw)
- Grinder with standard grinding bit
- Dremel™ Flex-shaft with 5/64" (2 mm) hollow core diamond drill bit
- Plastic bowl lined with micro-foam and enough water to cover the foam 3/8" (1 cm)
- Skewer 3/64" (1.2 mm) (or small metal rod)
- Flush cutter (Wire cutter)
- Flat nose pliers
- Round nose pliers
- Needle nose pliers
- Watch tool (used to insert the watchband pins)

MATERIALS:

- Cabochon- 5/8" x 4" (1.6 x 10.2 cm) 1/8" (3 mm) thick see Preparing Cabochons page 14
- 21-gauge round half hard gold (or silver) wire
- A watch face complete with fittings and pins
- 10 glass beads 1/8" (3 mm) dia.
- 'Bar and loop' type clasp findings

Create the Cabochon Components:

1. First we need to create the strip cabochon. I recommend using extra thin glass for both layers of this project. Glass that is only 1/16" (2 mm) thick will produce a watchband that is much lighter and more refined. Use a solid color glass for the bottom layer and cut a piece of glass approximately 5/8" x 4" (1.6 x 10.2 cm). Next cut a piece the same size for the top layer. Give the watchband some zing by using a piece of dichroic glass, dichroic frit or clear patterned dichroic glass. Stack these two layers and full fuse them in the kiln at 1450 °F to 1500°F (790°C - 815°C) see page 19 for more information.

Photo at above right illustrates the various stages of this cabochon production process.

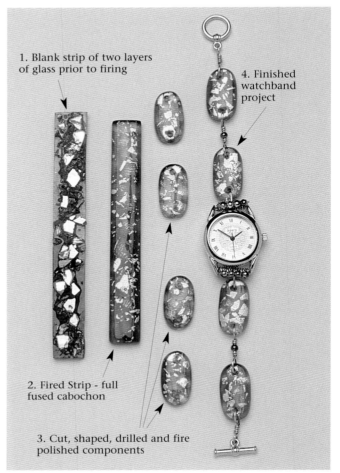

1. Blank strip of two layers of glass prior to firing

4. Finished watchband project

2. Fired Strip - full fused cabochon

3. Cut, shaped, drilled and fire polished components

This photo shows the four sequential stages of the project. In the last chapter we covered all the basic steps needed for accomplishing each one of these stages, so you may refer back if you need to. Yet you can see how these basic techniques can accomplish so many varying and exciting results.

2. Tip: Cut several watchband strips in different combinations and fuse them all at the same time. This will give you a variety to choose from and will save time the next time you choose to build watchband.

3. When you have your basic strip fused and ready to go measure and mark it (with a felt pen) into four equal pieces. Use a glass cutter to score and break or use a glass saw to cut the strip at the marks. Now grind and shape the pieces into ovals, or simply round the corners, or angle the corners to make elongated octagons, design whatever shape you like just make sure all four pieces the same size and shape. Each component should be approximately 1/2" x 1" x 1/8" thick (13 x 25 x 3 mm).

4. Now use the Dremel™ Flex-shaft with 5/64" (2 mm) bit to drill a hole at both ends of each component. Follow the same drilling procedure as described on page 34.

5. Fire Polishing: After cutting, shaping and drilling you'll need to fire-polish the four glass components (at approximately 1325°F to 1500°F (720°C to 815°C) see page 19). This extra firing will polish the edges and drilled openings for a professional high gloss finish.

Wire Wrapping:

6. Cut a 7" (18 cm) length of the 21-gauge half hard gold (or sterling silver) wire.

7. Pick up the first glass component and thread the wire through one of the drilled end holes.

8. Pull the wire through until the glass component is in the center of the wire.

9. Bend both the front and back wires up until they are parallel to one another.

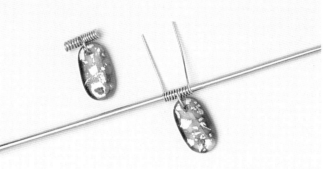

10. Place the 3/64" (1.2 mm) skewer horizontally between these two wires. It is IMPORTANT that the skewer is resting directly on the glass, DO NOT cross the wires over the glass prior to placing the skewer.

11. Wrap the wire that is behind the skewer toward you for two turns around the skewer. Then wrap the front wire away from you for two turns around the skewer. You will have formed two small coils.

12. At this point we need to compress the coils very tightly together. Use your needle nose pliers to grasp both lateral ends of the coils on the front side of mandrel and squeeze them together into one tight unit.

13. Move the pliers to the back of the mandrel and repeat this step. By doing this from both the front and the back, it assures that each coil is as tight as it can be and compensates for the angle of the pliers' jaws.

Note: This coil is going to house the watch pin that will connect the band to the watch itself. This means the coil needs to be the same length as the watch pin. Continue to coil the wire around the mandrel making certain that the coil has an equal amount of turns on either side, until the coil unit is the correct length. Check the coil width against the watch face (or the pins). Finish the coil by compressing it one more time before removing the mandrel. Since you need two of these to connect the watchband, repeat the above process on another one of the glass components.

14. The components may need to be adjusted to fit into the watch face correctly. For a final fitting, turn the watch face upside down, remove the pins and set them aside. Try fitting the coil unit into the watch. If it is too long simply clip an equal amount of the coil from either end using the tip of your flush cutters.

15. The next step is to join one of the components with the coiled wire to one of the two remaining drilled components. We will do this using a simple loop technique.

16. Measure and cut a 4" (10 cm) piece of wire. Grasp the wire with the flat nosed pliers approximately 1-1/2" (4 cm) down the wire and bend a 90° angle.

17. Now use the round nose pliers and insert the bent wire into the jaw so that one end of the wire is pointing down and the other end is to the right. (The photo shows how the wire would appear if you were looking at someone else's work). You will be looking at the pliers from the other end and the wire will be extending out to the right at the 3 o'clock position. Grasp the wire at the 3 o'clock position and bend it up and over the top jaw of the pliers to a 9 o'clock position, thus forming the first part of the loop (the photo at right shows what this first part of the loop looks like).

Tip: This loop must be large enough to accommodate the glass component so that it has free movement. The size of the loop is determined by the position of the wire on the round nose pliers, thus the further back in the jaw the larger the loop and vise-versa. Take this into account when placing the wire.

18. Now slide the wire from the upper jaw of the round nose pliers, and slide it back on the lower jaw. Continue to wrap the wire down and around the lower jaw until it has reached back to the 3 o'clock position (from your point of view).

19. Thread one the glass components that has a coil onto the wire and into the loop. (It doesn't matter if you insert it from the back or the front.)

20. Grasp the wire loop with the tip of the round nose pliers tight against the glass. Close off the loop by wrapping the shorter end of the wire around the longer end. Wrap it tightly for 2 revolutions. This will form a small coil wrap. Clip the excess wire from the wrap end with your wire cutters and crimp it neatly with your needle nose pliers.

21. Thread one of the glass beads onto the wire. (The beads may be used to make wrist size adjustments, add more beads for extra length or eliminate them to tighten the band.)

22. Now we are going to use the same technique to form the loop on the other end of the wire (steps 16-18). Grasp the extending wire with the tip of your needle nose pliers tight against the bead and bend it to a 90° angle. Insert the bent wire into the jaw of your round nose pliers so the bead or component end of the wire is pointing down and the other, "wire only" end, is to pointing to the 3 o'clock position.

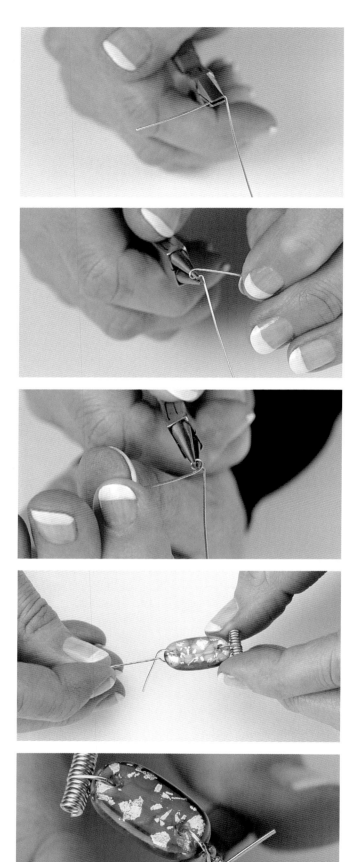

23. Grasp the wire at the 3 o'clock position and bend it up and over the upper jaw of the pliers to form the first part of the loop. Slide the wire from the upper jaw of the round nose pliers, move it to the lower jaw and slide it back on. Now continue to wrap the wire down and around the lower jaw until it has reached back to the 3 o'clock position.

24. Thread one of the 2 remaining unwired glass components onto this loop wire. This time is will make a difference if you insert it from the back or the front. You need to make sure both components are facing the same direction.

25. Grasp the wire loop with the tip of the round nose pliers tight against the glass (as we did in step 20) and close off the loop by wrapping the wire two revolutions toward the bead. This will form another small coil wrap. Clip excess wire from the wrap end with your wire cutters and crimp it neatly with your needle nose pliers. Don't forget to crimp this securely so that it will not scratch the wearer, snag clothing or begin to 'unravel'.

26. Install the Clasp: Attach a clasp to the remaining end of this assembly. I like to use a bar and loop clasp (also known as a toggle clasp) for these watchbands. Cut off another 4" (10 cm) piece of 21-gauge round wire and repeat steps 22 to 25.

27. You may want to add another bead to the band at this point. Whether it is necessary or not will depend on how large (or small) you need the watchband to be. After adding the bead (or not) you need to form another loop using the same technique as in the previous steps, but this time make the loop smaller (farther out on the round jaw pliers) because you will use it to attach to the "bar" finding.

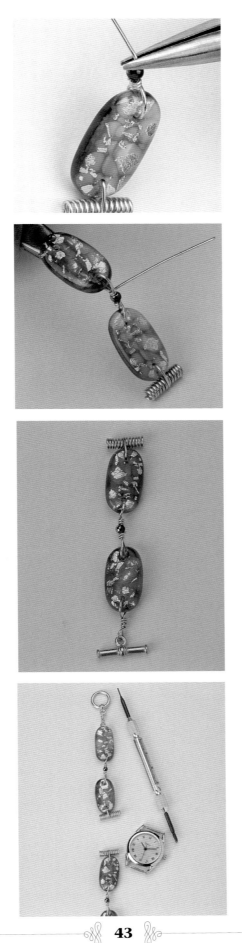

28. You have now completed one side of your watchband. You need to repeat this same final procedure for the other half, or "loop" of your watchband

29. Attach your new band to the watch face by inserting the pins through coils and use the "watch tool" to attach them as you would any type of watchband. I have found that it is easier to put the watch on your wrist if the bar part of the clasp is placed at the "bottom" of the watch.

30. You will notice that I have added a final decorative touch to the watch shown in the photo below. Simply thread four beads onto a piece of the 21 gauge wire, forming a hook on each end and attaching it to the coil. This is purely decorative and will not affect the 'structure' of the piece if you decide not to do this on your watchband. The finished watch measures approximately 7-1/2". Measure your wrist's circumference before beginning and if your wrist is smaller or larger, you may want to make adjustments as you go along. Adjustments can be as simple as adding or leaving off some of the small glass beads, using longer or shorter cabochons or leaving a little extra wire length on the 'bar and loop' clasp ends.

Bead Watchband

TOOLS:

- Flush cutters (Wire cutters)
- Needle nosed pliers
- Round Nosed pliers

MATERIALS:

- 21-gauge half hard round sterling silver or gold wire
- 4 fish beads (or something similar, approximately _" to 1" in length)
- Watch face (for bead bracelets) with single connection points
- 3-mm glass beads
- Bar and loop clasp findings

This project is very similar to the watchband in the previous project (page 40). The difference is this watchband uses glass beads instead of fused glass cabochons. There is a slight advantage to using beads since it is not necessary to drill holes in each segment. Glass beads are built on a mandrel and that means a central hole is already there! If you would like to use another type of bead other than glass, go ahead! There are so many beautiful beads around… use whatever inspires you!

Note: The watch face mechanism used in this next project is a type that is designed specifically for beaded bracelets. Notice that it only has a single connection point on each side for any beaded 'band' you might create. Watch faces also come with a single connection point at the top to be used for hanging pendant watches. Components like these are available through many craft retailers and jewelry supply distributors.

Fish Bead Watchband

The fish beads used for this project were created by Don McKinney especially for this project. Thanks, Don!

As you can see by studying the photographs at the top of this page, many different type of beads can work with this method (flat ones do work better). Time to go shopping again! (See... this book is filled with fun things to do!)

Here we see all the components placed together in the order they will be assembled

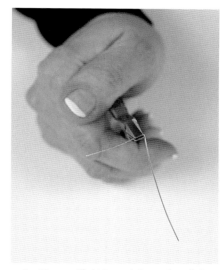

1. Cut a 4" (10 cm) length of the 21 gauge half hard round wire, and put a 90° angle bend at 1 1/2" (4 cm) from one end.

2. Form the top of the loop with your round nose pliers. (This is the same looping process as in project 5, steps 15-20 on page 42).

3. Finish the loop on the bottom jaw of your round nose pliers.

4. Attach the loops to the watch face, just as you did to the 'middle' cabochons in the last project.

5. Hold the loop close to the attachment point with the round nose pliers and wrap a coil tightly using the needle nose pliers. Clip off any excess wire and crimp the end of the coil so nothing protrudes.

6. Thread one of the small glass beads (or 2 depending on the wrist sizing) then thread the first major bead and finish with one more small bead.

Tip: If your 'major' beads are smaller, add another one to make each side a 3 bead design to achieve the proper length.

7. Repeat the steps to form the next loop.

8. Wrap the coil and close it off as you have done before. Clip off the excess wire and again crimp the coil tightly.

9. Start a new loop with another 4" (10 cm) length of wire. Repeat the steps (1 to 5) to form the loop and coil. Add this new loop to first bead unit wrap the coil and close it off as we've done before.

10. Add the second group of beads (one small, one major, one small)

11. Repeat the loop procedure (steps 1 - 5). Clip off excess wire and crimp the end of the coil.

12. Add the last set of beads and end with the toggle clasp.

13. Here we see the final assembly for one side of the watch. Repeat all these instructions for the other side of the watch ending with the loop end of the clasp.

Bracelets
Chapter 9

This chapter will show you how to create beautiful and unique gold and silver bangle bracelets, using eight square wires to form the wristband. The first project featured in this section is designed using gold wire and a fused cabochon for the center element. The second project is a variation created with silver wire and a special fish bead designed exclusively for this book by Arizona glass artist, Don McKinney.

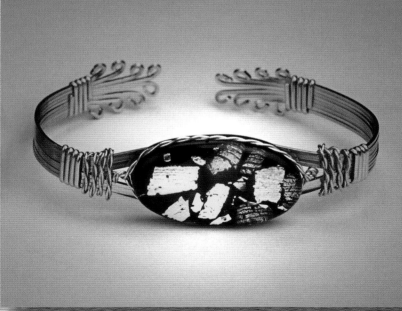

Bracelets
Chapter 9

Innovative Adornments

Bracelets
Chapter 9

Cabochon Bangle Bracelet

TOOLS:

- Grinder with jewelry bit
- Drill for twisting wire
- Flat nosed pliers
- Flush Cutters (Wire cutters)
- Metal ruler
- Felt tip marker
- Round nose pliers
- Quilter's tape
- Small pocket knife (with a dull blade) or a small flat-head screwdriver.

MATERIALS:

- Cabochon, oval, two layers full fused, 3/16" (5 mm) thick by 1/2" x 1 1/4" (1.3 x 3.2 cm)
- Gold (or Silver), half-hard:
  - -18 gauge half-round wire
  - -21 gauge square wire
  - -24 gauge round wire

With this project we are going to use techniques we have learned in the very first project, plus some new tricks with wire.

We used an oval cabochon for this sample bracelet but any shape cabochon could work just as well. Study the bracelet examples presented in the gallery photos (pages 47 to 49) to see the range of cabochon shapes and wire combinations that are possible.

1. Use your grinder fitted with the jewelry bit to create a channel in the side of the glass cabochon around its perimeter (see page 30, step1).

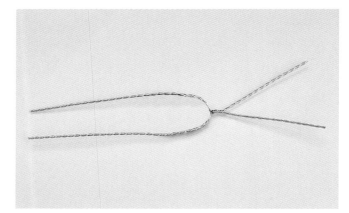

2. Next, cut two 12" (30 cm) pieces of 24-gauge round wire. Use the drill to twist them together (see page 24 for more details). Cut this twisted wire into two equal pieces approximately 5 1/2" (14 cm) long.

3. Lay these two twisted wires across one another, at a point approximately 2" (5 cm) from one end, and twist them together two times.

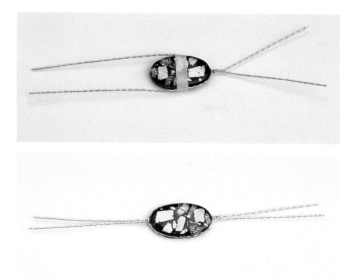

4. Spread the two longer ends of the wires apart at the twist and insert the cabochon into this 'U' notch, making sure the wires are securely set into the perimeter channel on both sides of the glass.

5. Wrap these wires half way around the cabochon and tape in place at the center of the cabochon (as shown in the photograph above right). Continue to

wrap the wire around to the other end of the glass. Check the wire to make certain it is seated properly in the channel, then pinch the wires together on the far side of the cabochon with needle nose pliers and secure them by twisting two times.

6. The above photo shows the finished assembly for this portion of the project. Set it aside for now.

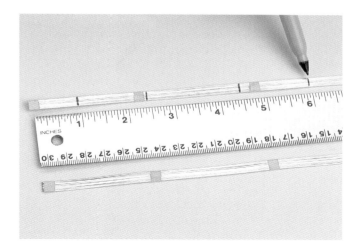

7. Cut eight pieces of 21-gauge square wire exactly 7" (18 cm) long and one piece of 18 gauge half round wire that is 12" (30 cm) long. Lay the eight square wire strips flat on your table side by side and tape them together at both ends and at 2 or 3 other areas along the length (you could tape in more places along the length if needed).

8. Mark four points on this group of wires with your felt tip pen. Starting left to right, place a mark at the 1" point, the 2 1/2" point, the 4 1/2" point and the 6" point (2.5, 6.4, 11.4, 15.2 cm). If you inadvertently wrapped tape around the wire at any of these points you will need to move the tape to one side.

9. The next step is to wrap the half round wire around the square wires at the indicated points to create a secure bundle.

Important Note: Make absolutely certain that the flat side of the "half-round" wire is on the inside of the wrap, against the square wires.

10. To begin wrapping, place the half round wire under the bundle (flat side facing up) at a very slight angle (so the wrap will be tight, but not overlapping on itself) with 1/8" (3 mm) extending past the bundle. Grasp both the half round wire and the bundle firmly with the tip of your flat nose pliers.

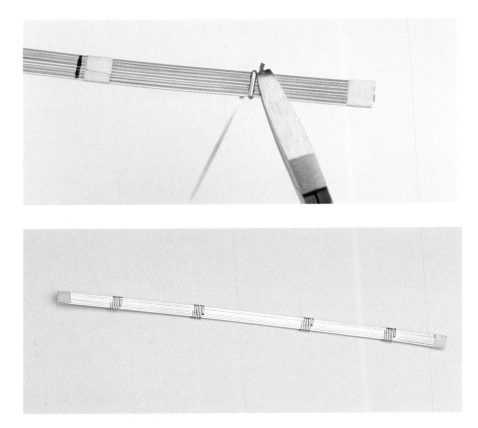

11. Begin wrapping the half-round wire by pulling it toward you from under the bundle then back up and around until you have created 4 complete revolutions. Clip the wire, leaving 1/8" extending on the opposite side from where you began the wrap. Now fold both these tail ends up and over the bundle and crimp the half-round wire to tighten and secure. If necessary, also crimp from the sides, as we did with the watchband coils (see page 41, steps 12 & 13) to ensure the half-round wire coil is tight against itself.

12. Repeat this wrapping process at each of the remaining 3 marks. When all four points are bundled with the half round wire you can remove the tape from the center area, but leave the tape on both ends for now.

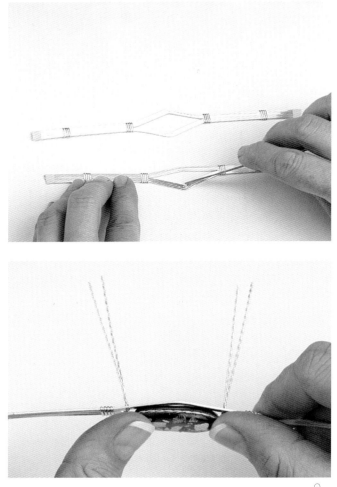

13. Use your ruler to find the exact center of the bracelet assembly and mark that spot. Use the dull pocketknife or small flat-head screwdriver to spread the two groups of wires apart at the center point. Insert the knife blade carefully between the two center wires until it has gone all the way through. Hold the assembly securely with one hand and begin to spread one side by applying outward pressure until the wires have bent approximately 1/4" from center. Now apply pressure with your blade on the other half until it has bent the same amount in the opposite direction.

Tip: If you are having a problem bending all four wires at once, try bending the 2 outside wires first, and then bend the next 2 wires.

The total spread needs to be slightly smaller than the width of the cabochon you are using, be sure to make the spread adjustment accordingly.

14. Now we're ready to combine this bracelet wristband assembly with the glass cabochon that we wire framed earlier (in steps 1-6). Bend the extending ends of the 4 wires on the cabochon down towards the back of the glass to almost 90°. Next insert these cabochon wires through the opening we just made in the bracelet's center as shown. Make sure you insert the wires from the front of the bracelet wristband (you can tell by looking at the half round bundling wires we wrapped in steps 11 and 12).

15. Hold the cabochon firmly in the center of the bracelet opening and begin to wrap the wires around the bracelet. Wrap the first wire up and over in one direction and wrap the second wire up and over in the opposite direction. One wire will wind toward the cabochon and the other one will wind toward the first bundling wire. Wind each wire two revolutions around the bracelet.

16. Repeat this process for the wires at other end of the cabochon. Finally use the flush cutters to trim each wire on the backside of the bracelet. Use your needle nose pliers to crimp these wires flat against the underside to ensure the ends cannot scratch your wrist.

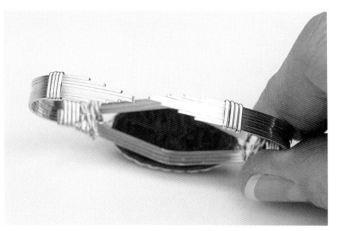

17. Now we need to form the wire assembly into a bracelet shape. You could form it on a bracelet mandrel or shape it with your fingers then use your own wrist to refine the final profile. Or use flat nose pliers as described in the next project on page 56.

18. When you have achieved a shape that is to your liking remove the tape from both ends. Next use the flush cutters to carefully trim the square wires in a step pattern as shown in the photograph. Each step is approximately 1/8" (3.2 cm) further up the bracelet.

19. For a final touch we are going to form the decorative scroll loops. Use your round nose pliers to bend four wires in one direction and four in the opposite direction as shown in the photograph. Try to make each curl exactly the same size.

20. This photograph illustrates how the finished bracelet should look from both the back view and front view.

Bead Bangle Bracelet

TOOLS:

- Flat nosed pliers
- Flush Cutters (Wire cutters)
- Metal ruler
- Felt tip marker
- Round nose pliers
- Masking tape
- Small pocket knife (with a dull blade) or small flat-head screwdriver

MATERIALS:

- Bead, approximately 1" x 3/4" (2.5 x 2 cm)
- Silver (or Gold), half-hard:
  - 21 gauge square wire
  - 18 gauge half-round wire
  - 24-gauge round wire

We are going to apply the same technique to form the wristband for this bracelet as we did the previous project. The variation is the use of a glass bead rather than a cabochon. Almost any bead can be adapted to a bracelet using this method but the best beads to use are flat and slightly longer than they are wide. When selecting a bead hold it on your wrist to see if it is an appropriate size and shape for a bracelet.

Glass artist (and good friend) Don McKinney made this whimsical tropical fish bead

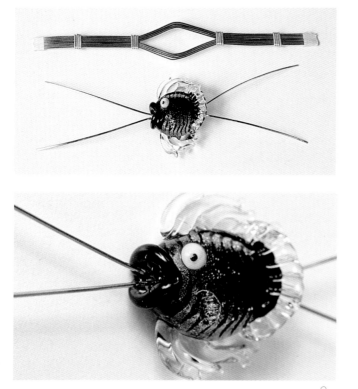

1. The wire wristband portion of this project is created using the same method as the previous project, Cabochon Bangle Bracelet. Follow the fabrication process as described in steps 7 through 13 on pages 51 & 52. When you have completed the flat-formed wire wristband set it aside. The fish bead I have selected for this project is approximately 1" x 3/4" (2.5 x 2 cm) but you could use almost any bead that is a suitable size to fit a person's wrist. Just make sure to spread wires the correct width to fit the bead you have selected.

2. Cut two pieces of 18-gauge half round wire 6" (15 cm) long. Place these two wires together and thread them through the middle of the bead until an equal amount is extending from both ends.

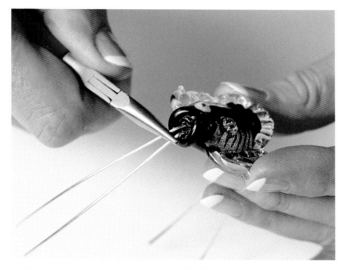

3. Bend the wires towards the back of the bead until they are about 90° angle. Do this on both ends.

4. Insert these wires into the center space in the wire wristband (as we in the last project, step 14).

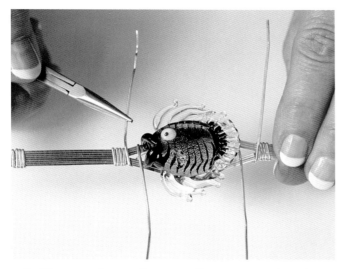

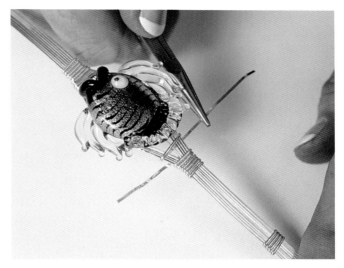

5. Now use the needle nose pliers to wrap the wires on each end of the bead by bending them in opposite directions and bring them up and around to the front of the bracelet.

6. Continue to wrap the wires around the bracelet 2 or 3 complete revolutions. One set of wire wraps will work toward the bead and the other will wrap toward the first wire bundle on the wristband.

7. Make sure to wrap this bundle tightly, but don't apply so much pressure that you risk damaging the glass bead.

Use the flush cutters to trim the wires. Then use flat nose pliers to compress the bundle (as we did on page 52, step 11) and finish by crimping the wire ends tightly. Repeat this wrapping process for the other end of the bead.

8. Now we need to form the bangle shape. In the last project you were instructed to form the bracelet on your wrist or on a bracelet mandrel. Another way is to use flat nosed pliers. First wrap masking tape around the wire wrapped areas on both ends of the bead to prevent them from moving. Securely grasp the end of the wire bundle by placing the pliers jaws at a 90° angle to the bundle. Now hold the bracelet with in one hand (fairly close to the bead) as you slowly but firmly twist the pliers and draw the bracelet around into a semi circle shape. Repeat this process for the other end of the bracelet wires.

9. Finally, grasp the bracelet in your hands and make minor adjustments until you are satisfied with the shape.

10. Finish the bracelet ends with decorative scroll loops as we did in the previous bangle bracelet project. See page 53, steps 18 & 19.

This photo (at left) is a sister bracelet to the one we just finished. This one has a similar fish bead and uses Gold wire.

Pins & Brooches
Chapter 10

Allow yourself to be inspired by the examples shown in this gallery section. Learn the easy techniques in this chapter and then create your own variations on the Angel Pin! So many of us cherish the thought of angels watching over us. This is why angels are such enormously popular symbols and desirable designs in jewelry.

Pins &
Brooches
Chapter 10

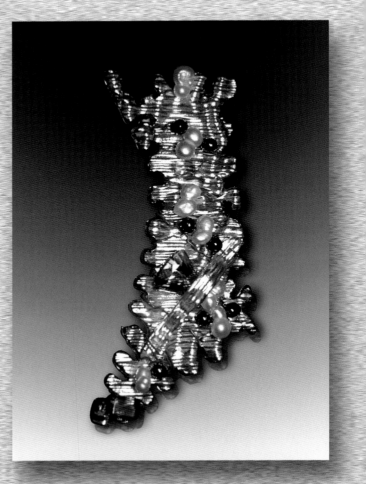

Pins &
Brooches
Chapter 10

Angel Pin Brooch

TOOLS:

- Grinder with channeling bit
- Drill for wire twisting
- Quilter's tape
- Metal ruler
- Flush Cutters (Wire cutters)
- Needle nose pliers
- 3/8" (10 mm) dowel

MATERIALS:

- Cabochon, oval, two layers full fused glass, 1/2" x 1 1/2" (1.3 x 3.8 cm)
- 24 gauge round gold-filled wire, half-hard
- 1 bead or pearl 5/16" (8 mm) diameter
- 4 beads or pearls 3/16" (5 mm) diameter

This is such a fun project, I don't think you'll mind if 'someone' is looking over your shoulder while you're working on it!

These three angel brooches were all created using the wire wrapping technique explained in this project.

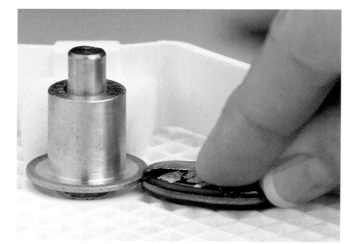

1. Use your grinder fitted with the Mika jewelry bit (see page 12) to grind a channel around the entire perimeter edge of the glass cabochon (see page 24 step 1 for more details).

2. Measure the outside perimeter of the glass using Quilter's tape (see page 28 step 2 for more details), add 3" (8 cm) to this measurement and cut two pieces of 24-gauge round wire to this length.

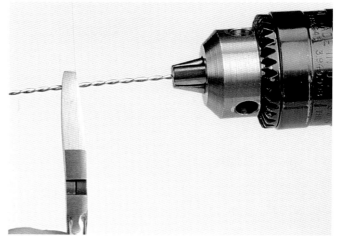

3. Put the wires together and insert one end into the drill chuck and tighten to hold the wire firmly and use the needle nose pliers to hold the opposite ends of the wire. Use the drill at a very low speed to twist them together (see page 31 step 3 for more details).

Innovative Adornments

4. Seat the twisted wire into the channel by placing the bottom of the cabochon at the center of the wire then bend the wires up and around the perimeter edge of glass. Use the needle nose pliers to pinch the wires together at the top of the glass then twist the angel's body 1-1/2 to 2 revolutions at the most, to secure the wire. You will now have two wires extending about 1" (2.5 cm) at the top of the cabochon. Wrap one of the wires around the other three times. This will form the angel's neck. Thread the larger bead on the vertical wire to make sure this 'head' bead rests on top of the neck wrap wire. If the hole is too large and it slips over, simply wrap another turn or 2 until the neck wrap is wider than the bead hole. Remove the head bead, clip the excess wire from the wrap and crimp the end so that it is not able to scratch or snag.

5. Now replace the head bead and form the halo. Take the wire extending from the bead, and wrap it around the dowel as shown in the photograph. After forming the halo, secure it by wrapping the wire two times below the halo (see photo at right). Clip the excess wire and crimp.

6. Next, measure, cut and twist two 7" (18 cm) long pieces of 24-gauge round wire together. Do this step four times to make a total of 4 twisted wires that we will use for the wings. Line up the center point of one of the twisted wires on the back of the neck just above the cabochon. Wrap one end of the wire completely around the neck and return to starting position.

7. Do the same with the remaining three twisted sections of wire, adding them to the neck, each one just above the last.

8. Cut one 4" (10 cm) long piece of 24-gauge round wire (single strand only – not twisted) and secure all the wing wires at the back of the neck with this wire. Put a gentle bend in the middle of this wire and loop it around the wings as shown. Use the needle nose pliers to twist it two to three times and then clip the excess wire and crimp.

9. Grasp the angel's neck at back of the wings with round nose pliers and bring the eight wing wires (four on each side) around to the front of the angel. Begin to shape the wings with your fingers or needle nosed pliers as shown in these 2 photographs.

10. Continue to hold the angel with the round nose pliers and coil the ends of the wings with the needle nosed pliers to add a softer look. As an alternative you could add a small bead to some or all of these coils if you like.

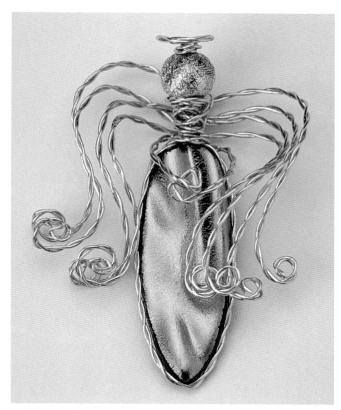

11. For the arms, measure, cut and twist two 4" (10 cm) long pieces of the 24-gauge round wire together. Wrap this wire around the neck just below the wings. Form a loop on the end of each wire for the hands.

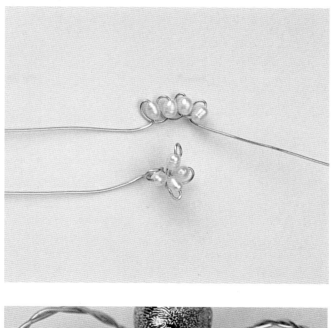

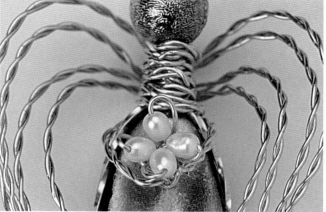

12. To make a 'flower' for the angel to hold, thread four small beads or pearls onto another 4" long section of 24-gauge round wire (single strand only). Loop the wire around each pearl to serve as the petals. Bring the four petals together and twist the wires to form the flower as shown.

13. Insert the flower stem into the loops that form the hands. Twist the extending stem wire around the lower hand to secure it and clip any excess wire.

14. This photograph (at left) shows the finished wire wrapped project. You'll still need to attach a brooch pin-clasp onto the angel's back. The easiest way to do this is to use an adhesive such as Bond 527 or E6000 (refer to page 25 for more information on adhesives) and let the adhesive air dry.

Rings
Chapter 11

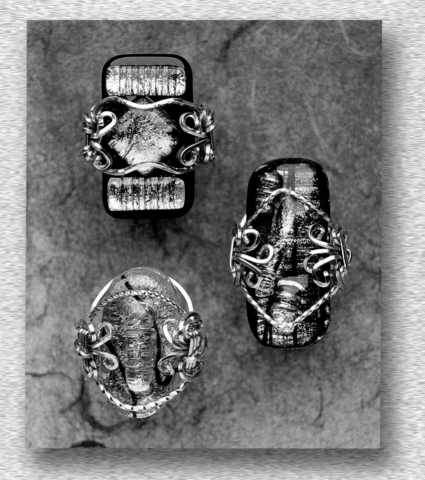

Wire wrapped rings are beautiful, as you can readily see. While the technique can be considered a miniature version of the bangle bracelet (in Chapter 9), it is a bit more complicated. We have all discovered somewhere in our craft experience that working smaller is rarely easier! Creating rings in this manner will require manipulating seven wires and a very skillful assembly. This would be considered an advanced project. It is best to comfortably master the bangle bracelet before attempting the wire wrapped ring, but it will definitely be worth the effort once you do!

Rings
Chapter 11

Wire Wrapped Cabochon Ring

TOOLS:

- Flat nosed pliers
- Needle nose pliers
- Flush Cutters (Wire cutters)
- Quilter's tape
- Ring mandrel
- Metal ruler
- Felt tip marker
- Round nose pliers
- Masking tape
- Small pocket knife (with a dull blade) or small flat-head screwdriver

MATERIALS:

- Cabochon, oval, two layers full fused, 3/16" (5 mm) thick by 1/2" x 3/4" (1.3 x 1.9 cm)
- Gold (or Silver), half-hard:
    - 21 gauge square wire
    - 18 gauge half-round wire
    - 24 gauge round wire

We have all discovered somewhere in our craft experience that working smaller is rarely easier! Creating rings in this manner will require manipulating seven wires and a very skillful assembly. This would be considered an advanced project. It is best to comfortably master the bangle bracelet before attempting the wire wrapped ring, but it will definitely be worth the effort once you do!

This ring cleverly uses the wire-wrapping process to capture and hold the cabochon without having to grind a channel, drill a hole or use any adhesives.

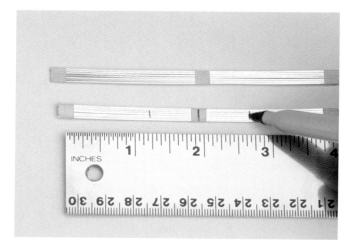

1. Before we begin this project I recommend that you review the fabrication process for the wristband in the Bangle Bracelet on page 51 & 52 steps 7 to 13.

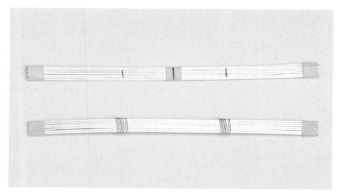

2. Measure and cut seven 4" (10 cm) strips of 21-gauge square wire. Lay the seven strips of 21-gauge wire side by side then tape the ends and middle. Calculate and mark the exact center point of the bundle. Measure and mark a point on either side of the center point that is 3/4" (2 cm) to both the left and right of the center mark.

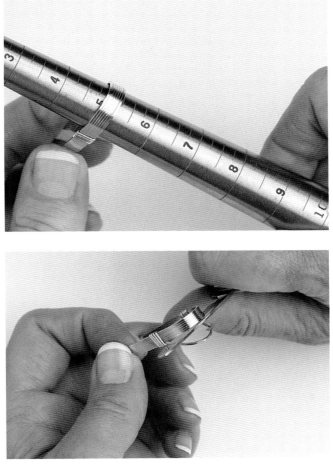

3. Cut a 6" (15 cm) length of the 18 gauge half round wire. Use this wire to wrap the wire bundle at each of these 2 marked locations. Hold the shank and the half round wire with your flat nosed pliers (the same way we did in the Bangle Bracelet Project on page 51 & 52) and make 3 or 4 wraps around the shank. Cut the excess wire and crimp together securely. Repeat for the other mark.

4. Use the ring mandrel to bend the flat ring shank into the correct shape. I have found it is helpful to position the ring on the mandrel at the mark that is two sizes smaller than needed then allow the wires to spring back slightly to the correct size.

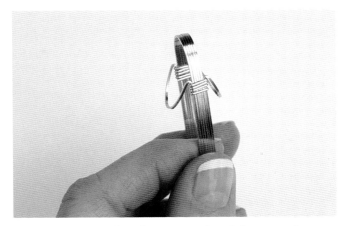

5. Use the small pocket-knife to separate the first wire from the main bundle.

6. Continue to bend it outward and down as shown in the photograph. Do the same to the outermost wire on the opposite side in the same manner.

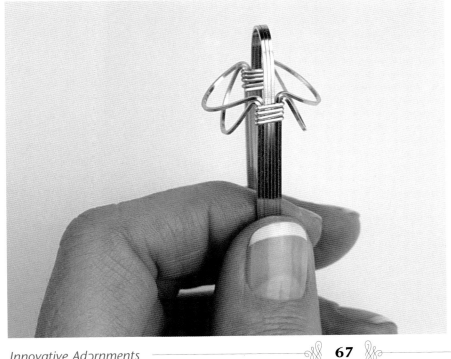

7. Repeat this bending process with second wire on both sides, but not to the same angle. Look closely at the photograph for the proper positions.

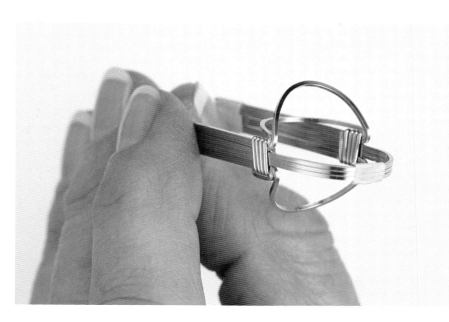

8. You should now have three wires left in the middle. These wires are the 'bottom' of the ring (the part that will wrap around your finger). Wrap these three wires tightly with masking tape to hold them together while we finish the rest of the ring.

9. Insert the glass component between the two bent wire sets. Undoubtedly you will have to make some adjustments to the wires to make sure the fit is precise and snug leaving the cabochon centered and balanced.

10. Tape the glass and wires securely together as you see in the illustration at right. The tape will hold the assembly securely while you are handling the ring through the next few steps.

11. Gently push the piece back onto the ring mandrel to check it for final sizing. Make any necessary adjustments by gently pressuring the shank 'tighter' or 'looser' with your fingers. Once you are satisfied with the size, remove the ring, turn it around and slide it back onto mandrel once again and repeat what you have just done. Since the ring mandrel is tapered this two-sided readjustment is needed to assure that the three wire elements are of the exact same shape and size.

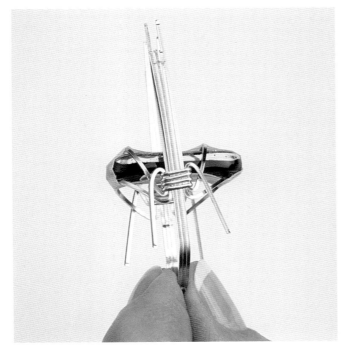

12. Remove the ring from the mandrel and grasp the ring by the bottom with one hand. Use your needle nose pliers to grab the end of one of the outside wires on a vertical shank and bend it away from the others keeping them parallel to the wire wraps. Bend it until it is pointing down, almost 180° from where it started. Do this for all four the wires on both sides of the cabochon.

13. Use the wire cutters to clip these wires to about a 1/8" (3 mm) overhang. Use your needle nose pliers to wrap these overhang wire ends around the glass-supporting wire (the one it's resting on) and into the cavity underneath the cabochon. Finally, crimp these wires securely.

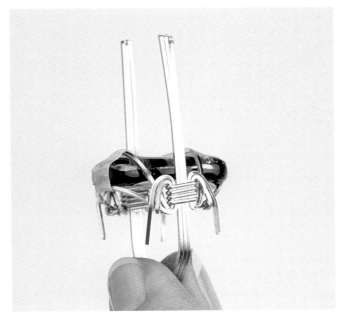

14. This photo shows how the ring should look after the first four wires have been bent and secured into the cavity below the cabochon. At this point it's a good idea to place the ring back on the mandrel to re-check the size.

15. Now bend the second (next) set of shank wires in the same manner as we did for the first set (steps 12-14). Take care to bend this set to follow on top of the first set. Neatness counts in jewelry making and this is one of those steps that can make a big difference between a good and a great jewelry piece.

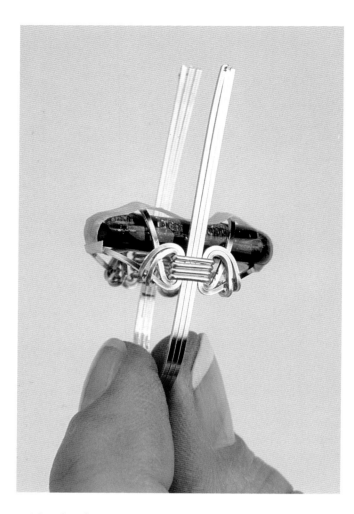

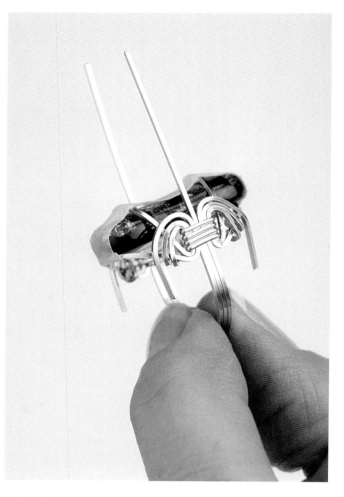

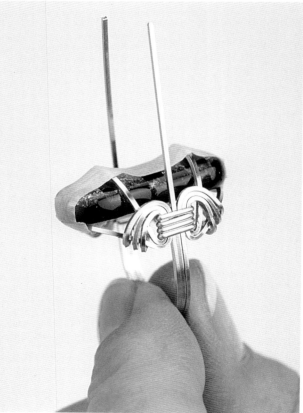

16. Clip these wires to about a 1/8" (3 mm) overhang and wrap the wire ends around the glass-supporting wire and into the cavity underneath the cabochon. Crimp these wires securely as you did with the first set. Notice in the photo how neatly these second wires flow along the top of the first wire.

17. Now bend the third and final set of shank wires in the same manner. Clip and wrap as we did with the first and second set of wires.

18. Repeat these steps for both sides of ring. You should have one final wire sticking up from the center of the bundle on both sides of the ring. This photo clearly shows how the ring should look after all wires have been bent, wrapped and crimped. Carefully study the way these wires all line up with one another and try to make yours follow this same pattern. This is where you can really make a professional difference in your work.

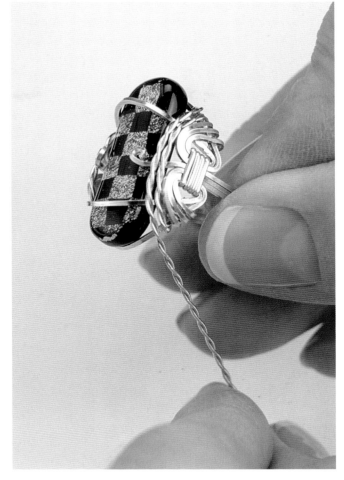

19. The ring is almost complete. Remove the masking tape that is covering the cabochon make sure that the glass is still being held firmly in place. Trim the remaining center wires to about 1/4" (6 mm) and form them into a decorative spiral. Finally bend them over the top of the glass cabochon so they lay flat as pictured.

20. The ring is now finished and you could simply clean it and wear it at this point. However if you wish you could wrap some twisted wire around the top (but under the cabochon) for an additional ornamental touch. This extra wire could be a contrasting color, for instance if you made your ring using gold wire use silver wire for the decorative add on.

All these rings were created using the wire wrapping technique as described in this project. Study each one to find its unique features

Earrings
Chapter 12

In this final chapter we'll discuss some of the methods I used to create the earrings shown on these gallery pages. As you can see earrings use simple variations on the techniques we covered in the previous chapters and many combine several processes into one project. Most of the surface décor on these earrings were attached using a method I like to call "cold-fusing", which is nothing more than applying elements using various adhesives. See page 25 for information on this cold-fusing process.

Innovative Adornments

Earrings
Chapter 12

Earrings
Chapter 12

Earrings
Chapter 12

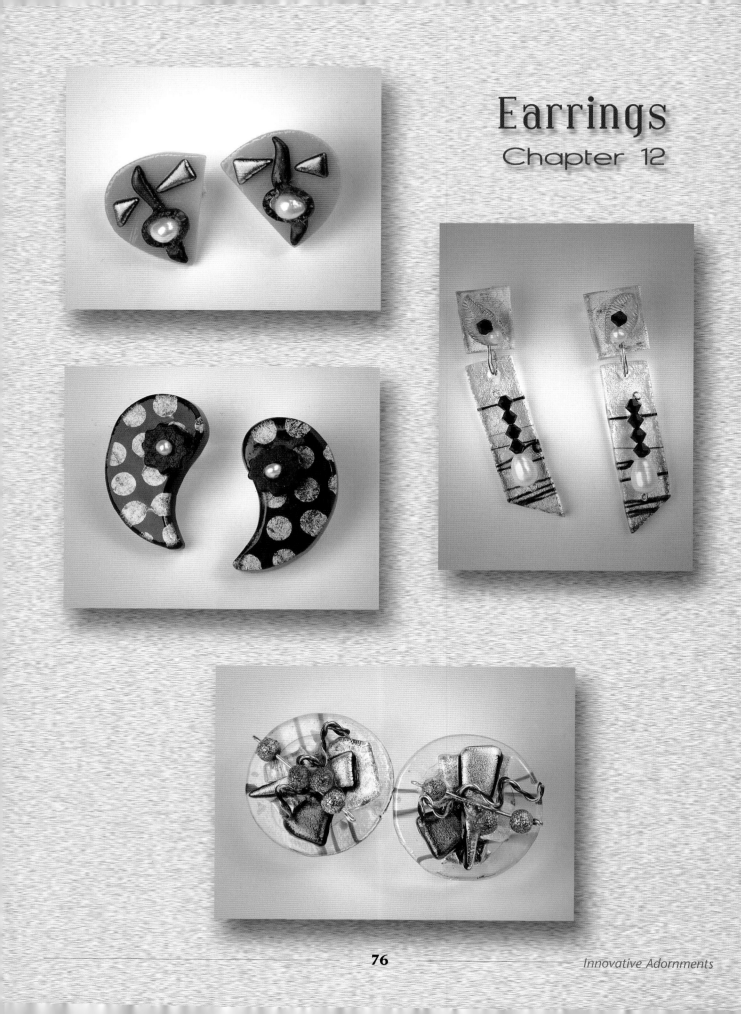

Earrings

The main thing to remember when designing earrings is they must weigh as little as possible. Ears can't hold much weight so I always use 1/16" (1.6 mm) thin glass and try to keep the design elements small as well. I use the cold fusing process (adhesives) extensively for my earrings, see page 25 for more

Dichroic Dangles With Pearls

I created this pair of earrings by cutting 2 pieces of thin dichroic glass approximately 3/8" x 1-1/8" (1 x 30 cm). I was careful to match the vertical stripe pattern on both blanks as I cut them (the stripe was already on the glass). Then I used my grinder to shape the outside edges to give them some interest and used my Dremel to drill 2 small holes for the wire. These pieces were then fire polished to smooth all edges. I used the Bond 527 adhesive (see page 25 for more details on adhesives) to attach 3 small irregular pearls to each one. The final step was to attach the glass dangles using 2 simple jump ring loops (I used 24 gauge half hard wire to make mine) to the stud findings that I purchased from my jewelry supplier. They came exactly as you see them here with the pearls, the loop and the studs (at the back) already to go.

Notched Dangles With Bead Loops

You should recognize the dangles on these earrings it's similar to chapter 7 - project 4 on page 36. These are single layer of thin dichroic glass about 3/8" x 7/8" (9.5 x 22 mm) notched, drilled and fire polished. The upper stud component is a commercial finding that I customized with 2 fire polished circles cut from the same glass. The dangles were attached to the upper stud part using the same loop technique we used for the watchband bracelet on page 42.

Tack Fuse Cabochon with Hanging Beads

This project uses 2 tack fused cabochons (see page 19 for details) that are approximately 5/8" x 3/4" (1.6 x 2 cm). I drilled 2 holes (large enough to receive 24 gauge wire) at the bottom corners of each one. I cut 2 pieces 1-1/2" (3.8 cm) of 24 gauge round, half hard, gold filled wire and threaded 7 small beads onto each wire. The wires were pushed through the holes in the cabochon from the back and then I used my smallest needle nose pliers to twist the ends into a spiral. The final step was to attach standard earring studs to the backs using E6000 adhesive (see page 25).

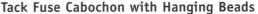

Index

A

Adhesives 25
Author Contact Information . . .4
Author - Message 4

B

Basic Glassworking 8
Bond 527 And E6000 25
Bracelet - Bead Bangle 54
Bracelet - Cabochon 50
Bracelets - Chapter 9 47
Breaking Pliers 10

C

Cabochon 14
Channeling Bit 12
Co-Efficient Of Expansion 6
Cold Fusing (Adhesives) 25
Compatible Glass 7
    What It Is 7
Copyright © 2002 2

E

Earrings - Chapter 12 72

F

Fusing Glass 6
    Dichroic Glass 6
    Standard Thickness 6
    Tested Compatible 6
    Thin Thickness 6
Fusing Levels 19
    Fire Polishing 19
    Full Fusing 19
    Tack Fusing 19

G

Glass Cabochons 14
    Cutting, Shaping, etc. 14
    Preparing 14
Glass Cutters 8
    Breaking Out The Score . . .10
    Gripping Styles 8
    Scoring The Glass 9
Glass Saws 13
    Bandsaws 13
    Tablesaws 13
    Wiresaws 13
Glass Snappers™ 10

Glass Tools & Supplies

Glass Tools & Supplies 8
Glassworking Pliers 10
Grinders And Bits 12

I

Introduction 6
    Getting Started 6

K

Kiln Firing Process 22
Kiln Safety Considerations 21
Kiln Set Up And Firing 17
Kiln - Choosing 17
Kiln Wash 18

M

Mika Jewelry Bit™ 12

P

Pendant - Channel Mount 30
Pendant - Hanging Loop 34
Pendant - Notched And Drilled 36
Pendant - Notched Channel . . .32
Pendants - Chapter 7 26
Pin - Angel 60
Pins & Brooches - Chapter 10 .57
Pliers - Glassworking 10

R

Ring - Wire Wrapped 66
Ring Mandrel 68
Rings - Chapter 11 64
Ringstar™ Runners 10

R

Safety Glasses 9

T

Table Of Contents 5
Tested Compatible 6
The Projects - Contents Page 5

U

Ultraviolet Cement 25

W

Watchband - Bead 44
Watchband - Cabochon 40
Watches - Chapter 8 38
Wire Wrapping Tools 23
    Beads 24
    Dowels 23
    Drill (Dremel™) 24
    Pre-Drilling Set-Up 34
    Drill (Standard) 24
    Special Note 34
    Flat Nose Pliers 23
    Flush Cutters 23
    Marking Pen 23
    Metal Ruler 23
    Metal Skewers 23
    Needle Nose Pliers 23
    Quilter's Tape 23
    Ring Mandrel 24
    Round Nose Pliers 23
    Short Nosed Scissors 23
    Watch Tool 23
    Wire (Assorted Types) 24
    Wire Cutters 23

Source
Wire Wrapping Supplies

To find a convenient distributor for the fusing glass, kilns, tools and other assorted wire wrapping supplies featured in the book please contact:

J. P. Glassworks Studio
50 North Vine Street
Hazleton, PA. 18201 USA
E-mail:
jayne@jpglassworks.com
Website:
www.jpglassworks.com

Pins &
Brooches

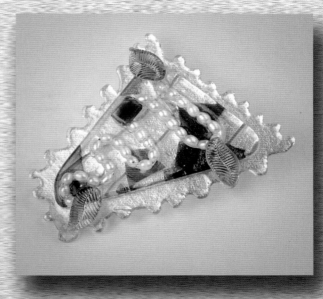

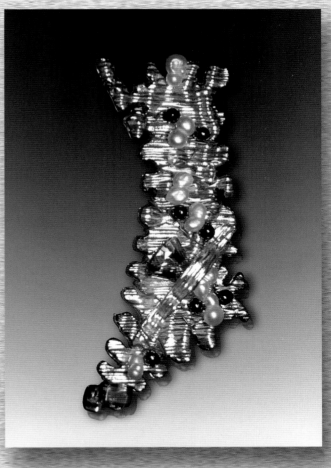

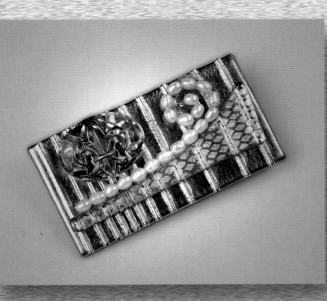

See page 57 - 59 for more
Pins and Brooches

Wardell
PUBLICATIONS INC

Instruction, Inspiration and Innovation for the Art Glass Communnity

Introduction to **Glass Fusing**
by Petra Kaiser

Fuse It
by Petra Kaiser

A Continuing Journey in Kiln Worked Glass

PATTERNS FOR *South Beach Frame*
for stained glass, fused glass & mosaic projects

Jayne Persico present *Innovative Adornments*
An Introduction to Fused Glass & Wire Jewelry

Jayne Persico present **Kiln Formed Bracelets**

Jayne Persico present *Glass Kiln Casting with Colour de Verre*

INTRODUCTION TO **PRECIOUS METAL CLAY**
By: Mary Ann Devos

PRECIOUS METAL CLAY In Mixed Media
Bringing It All Together
by Mary Ann Devos

Introduction to **Stained Glass**
A Step by Step Teaching Manual

QUICK SUCCESS STAINED GLASS
A BEGINNER'S INSTRUCTION GUIDE

art glass panel designs one

Orchids in Glass
by Chantal Paré

MAIDENS, MYTHS AND MERMAIDS
by Jody and Delray Shepard

IN FULL BLOOM
Patterns for 17 Stained Glass Windows
by Sabine Sehein

PATTERNS FOR **MIRRORS & FRAMES**

STAINED GLASS **WALL DECORATIONS**
PATTERNS FOR CLOCKS, MIRRORS AND PICTURE FRAMES
DESIGNS FOR 29 COMPLETE PROJECTS STEP-BY-STEP INSTRUCTION

STAINED GLASS **Clock Gallery**

Classic Alphabets
FULL-SIZED ALPHABETS & NUMERALS
Welcome

Windows of Elegance Volume 1

Windows of Elegance Volume 2

Windows of Mystique

WINDOWS FOR THE SOUL
by Ron Bovard

Bevel Window Designs

PATTERNS FOR **TERRARIUMS & PLANTERS**
DESIGNS FOR 30 COMPLETE PROJECTS GUIDE TO SELECTION AND CARE OF PLANTS STEP-BY-STEP INSTRUCTION

Stained Glass *Windows of Vision* Collection Four
Featuring Leslie Perlis Studio

Windows from a Different Perspective

Stained Glass *Windows of North America*

Windows of Enduring Beauty

Windows of Distinction
McMow Art Glass

Patterns for **Stained Glass BOXES**
FULL-SIZE PATTERNS FOR 11 ART GLASS BOXES

INTRODUCCIÓN AL VITRAL Manual Didáctico
Una guía manual completa sobre el vitral coloreado

FULL SIZE **LAMPSHADE PATTERNS I** FOR MINI TO MEDIUM SIZED SHADES

MORE **LAMPSHADE PATTERNS II** FOR 15" TO 22" DIAMETER SHADES

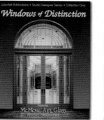

CHARLES KNAPP **DESIGNS FOR LAMPS**
PATTERNS FOR 18 SMALL TO MEDIUM SHADES

Charles Knapp **DESIGNS FOR LAMPS II**

NORTHERN SHADES

e-mail: info@wardellpublications.com   website: www.wardellpublications.com